The Death Penalty on Trial

CRISIS IN AMERICAN JUSTICE

Bill Kurtis

PublicAffairs

New York

Book design by Mark McGarry
Set in Minion

Library of Congress Cataloging-in-Publication data
The death penalty on trial : crisis in American justice / Bill Kurtis.—1st ed.
p. cm.
ISBN 1-58648-169-X
1. Capital punishment—United States. I. Title.
HV8699.U5K87 2004
364.66'0973—dc22
2004050564

FIRST EDITION
10 9 8 7 6 5 4 3 2 1

CONTENTS

Friday, January 10, 2003, was a turning point for American justice. It was a cold morning in Chicago. Lake Michigan heaved a thick, frosty breath over the city. The automobile arteries into the city's business core were already full. Traffic inched along as the elevated L-train rattled through a canyon of skyscrapers. The grinding of metal against metal had barely faded behind a passing train when a black van pulled alongside the curb in front of DePaul University Law School on Jackson Boulevard. Commuters rushed by, barely noticing as the governor of Illinois emerged from the vehicle, staff assistants and a state trooper trailing behind him. They couldn't have known the grave importance of Governor George Ryan's mission that day nor the agonizing journey that had led him to this speech at DePaul. Even his closest associates, while aware that the withering pressure had claimed the governor's sense of humor in the last few days, still did not know of his final decision.

In the few feet from the curb to the front door of the law school the party passed a newsstand. All the local papers carried the story. The *Chicago Sun-Times* quoted "sources" that said the governor would pardon some death row inmates in his last three days in office. The *Chicago Tribune* had also picked up the leak, but its columnists wondered if Ryan would go through with such a radical act. After all, such pardons would be unprecedented. No one could remember a governor ever doing anything like this. It would be a slap in the face of the entire justice system. Ryan would be declaring that America's entire system of lawyers, trial courts, and appellate courts built on centuries of English common law could not handle the job. He would be taking justice out of their hands and redefining it himself. Quite an act of bravado, especially for a non-lawyer.

The governor walked straight to the elevators, offering a quick and easy wave to the security guard. He had been a popular governor and would have easily won re-election but for a nagging litany of corruption charges during his tenure as Illinois secretary of state. This would be one of two final speeches in a long career in Illinois politics.

A sense of finality hung in the air as the group made its way down a corridor on the eighth floor. They entered the lecture hall. George Ryan strode from the back of the room down its sloping floor to a podium at the center, where he would stand like Cicero lecturing in an ancient amphitheater. Some fifty tables marched up around him in a tiered pattern, filled with young law students, many swiveling back and forth nervously on their attached seats.

Ryan looked up at their eager faces. He was an approachable, jolly sort of man. His short-cropped gray-white hair topped a round face giving him the warm look of a beloved grandfather. But today his face was rigid and serious. He frowned down at his notes. Then George Ryan took a deep breath and made history.

His first words from the podium, carried live on radio and recorded by an array of television cameras, made it clear that he had chosen to leave a remarkable legacy. He would pardon four inmates sitting on death row, he said, because, "It was the right thing to do."

"Three years ago," Ryan said. "I was faced with startling information. We had exonerated not one, not two, but thirteen men from death row. They were found innocent. Innocent of the charges for which they were sentenced to die. Can you imagine? We nearly killed innocent people. We nearly injected them with a cocktail of deadly poisons so that they could die in front of witnesses on a gurney in the state's death chamber. That's a pretty gruesome picture."

There was no ruling from the Illinois Supreme Court to back Ryan up, no opinion from the state's attorney general. This was the personal judgment of a former pharmacist and aging statesman who had come to his decision the hard way, as the final arbiter over the lives of men he might have to send to their deaths.

George Ryan had only two days left in his term. He could have escaped this difficult decision and driven off toward his hometown of Kankakee, Illinois, leaving the heavy responsibility to the next governor. But Ryan knew there was a serious problem with the Illinois system and that to walk away would have been a dereliction of duty. And so he chose to sign off as a whistleblower, knowing he would be pilloried by relatives of the victims of death row inmates, death penalty proponents, and many in law enforcement. He most likely did not know he would also be nominated for the Nobel Peace Prize and would win praise from governments and individuals around the world. Either way, his decision to speak out instead of remaining quiet was an act of immense courage.

Why did he do it? The short answer is that George Ryan felt deeply betrayed; the system of justice he had always trusted was not working and maybe never did work the way we all had been led to believe.

Governor Ryan recited the statistics for his audience: "Half of the nearly 300 capital cases in Illinois had been reversed for a new trial or re-sentencing. Nearly half!" he emphasized. "Thirty-three of the Death Row inmates were represented at trial by an attorney who had later been disbarred or at some point suspended from practicing law.

"I'm not a lawyer," he said, "but I don't think you need to be one to be appalled by those statistics. I have one question: How does that happen?"

The question was the cry of a layman who may not know the details of *habeas corpus* or be able to translate *res judicata*, but who has a common sense of right and wrong.

How does that happen?

What was happening in the process of determining the truth that prevented justice from prevailing? In an assembly plant, the foreman could check the robots or the individual parts being welded together. Quality control employees could stop the line if they detected anything amiss. If a defective product reached the end of the line the whole assembly might shut down to find and fix the problem. Why weren't such checks and balances working in death penalty trials? Why wasn't someone shutting down the line?

The governor's voice rose as the emotion of sleepless nights spilled out: "We had executed twelve people since capital punishment was reinstated here in Illinois in 1977. With the thirteenth exonerated inmate in January of 2000, we had released more innocent men from Death Row than those hopefully guilty people we had executed. Three years ago, I described it as a shameful scorecard. Truly shameful. So I did the only thing I could. I called for what is in effect a moratorium. A lot of people called that courageous. It wasn't. It was just the right thing to do. How do you let innocent people march to Death Row without somebody saying, 'Stop the show'?"

Three years before, George Ryan had stopped the show. And now, with this extraordinary act of gubernatorial pardon, he was assuring himself a place in the annals of American history. No other inmate had been pardoned while sitting on death row still appealing his case. Ryan pardoned four. And there was more to come.

The next day, January 11, under another cold Chicago sky, Governor George Ryan upstaged himself by commuting the death sentences of 164 other death row inmates, replacing the threat of execution with a sentence of life in prison without parole. Among those inmates were psychopathic killers, sexual predators, organized crime hit men, and the most deviant kinds of criminals. Their crimes challenge the imagination of how terrible and cruel one human can be to another. Jacqueline Williams cut the full-term fetus from the belly of a pregnant woman she and Fedell Caffey had killed because she wanted a baby. Although the baby lived and was kidnapped, the two other children of the victim were killed. Daniel Edwards lured Steve Small, the publisher of the *Kankakee Journal* newspaper, to the garage of a home he was renovating, stuffed him into the trunk of a car, and then buried him alive. Small was a neighbor who used to babysit for the Ryan children in the governor's hometown.

The governor was not deterred. In his pardon speech, he chided prosecutors for being overzealous, the state legislature for not passing death penalty reforms, and the legal profession in general for presiding over a system that could not be trusted. "If we haven't got a system that works then we shouldn't have a system," he said.

Some lawyers protested. They maintained that the system did not fail. The elaborate process of appeals and review by higher courts, they argued, would eventually find the errors and release the wrongfully convicted. But it takes an average of twelve years for a case to work its way through the process, which was one more reason Governor Ryan chose to circumvent the full legal process and pardon the death row inmates with only three days left in his term. Justice delayed is justice denied, he said.

Cook County State's Attorney Dick Devine took issue with Ryan's decision saying, "All of these cases would have been best left for consideration by the courts, which have the experience, the training, and the wisdom to decide innocence or guilt. Instead, they were ripped away from the justice system by a man who is a pharmacist by training and a politician by trade."

Governor Ryan stood fast. He had chosen a path few politicians have ever had the fortitude to tread, to stand tall in opposition to the legal establishment. And yes, it was all the more remarkable because he was not a lawyer but a citizen who saw injustice being committed and decided to stop it.

Inside the prisons throughout the state, word spread like news of a riot in the next cell block. Every inmate knew someone on death row. Every one had been condemned by the criminal justice system and could convincingly argue his innocence. This was a shock none of them had seen coming. For the first time, inmates in the general population actually envied those on death row.

The collateral damage was quickly tallied by the prosecutors whose staffs had worked hard to convict the residents of death row. They were doing their job, they argued, representing the families of the victims. Ryan was off his rocker. These were not innocent inmates like the seventeen wrongfully convicted who had been released. This was a blanket commutation. Those criminals deserved to be there.

State's Attorney Dick Devine, left holding obsolete files and worthless death sentences, described the governor's action as a breach of faith with the dead victims and called it "outrageous and unconscionable." Others held their fire, waiting to see if Ryan's move was just a desperate attempt to build a legacy in his final days of office, or whether it would be considered one of the great acts of courage in America's political history.

George Ryan's decision was all the more astonishing because he had been an advocate of the death penalty for twenty-six years while he served Illinois as a legislator, secretary of state, and lieutenant governor before taking office as Illinois' 39th governor in 1998. But something happened in 1998 prior to his oath of office. That was the year Ryan faced the statistics for the first time and fully realized that Illinois had released more men from death row than it had executed. Two years later, in January, 2000, the governor declared a moratorium on executions until a commission could review the system of capital punishment in Illinois. "Until I can be sure, with moral certainty, that no innocent man or woman is facing a lethal injection, no one will meet that fate," Ryan said. The blue ribbon commission went to work and Governor Ryan went about his business of governance.

In 1997, the legal profession was embarrassed publicly when some Northwestern University journalism students working on a class project asked a few simple questions about a trial. The students' project required them to re-interview a witness who had helped convict a homicide defendant and send him to death row. Their professor, David Protess, had a tip that the death row inmate was innocent and that the witness had lied on the stand. When the students and a private investigator conducted the interview the witness recanted her testimony and admitted that she had lied on the witness stand. The students went on to investigate other questionable cases and discovered witnesses who felt coerced into giving false testimony; evidence that had been hidden by prosecutors; and, most damning because it was irrefutable, DNA tests that exonerated the convicted.

The teaching technique pioneered by Professor Protess was cloned by Ed Bishop of Webster University near St. Louis. Bishop sent his students to interview a key witness in the death row case of Richard Clay, convicted in a 1994 killing. The witness in that case, a jailhouse informant, accomplice, and suspect in the killing, Chuck Sanders, told the students that prosecutors had told him to overstate the amount of prison time he'd be getting for his role in the murder-for-hire scheme when he was called as a prosecution witness to finger Richard Clay. Sanders told the jury he'd be going to jail for ten years when in fact he got a five-year suspended sentence. As a result of the students' findings, U.S. District Judge Dean Whipple ordered a new trial for Richard Clay, saying the state had violated Clay's rights by failing to disclose details of Sanders's "flexible or negotiable" plea deal. Would the error have been corrected within the legal system? Probably not. Witnesses are not automatically re-interviewed.

The Northwestern and Webster University students had pierced the veil. They had figured out how the system works and they had discovered that often it doesn't work properly. Journalism students had interviewed witnesses for class projects before, but they didn't have the impact of Protess's students. It was the DNA evidence that made the difference.

DNA provides evidence without bias because it reveals the unique pattern of chromosomes that exist within each human being's living cell. DNA is our individual code or blueprint of life. It's a marker of the unique identity of every person on earth. And it's contained in every cell, no matter how minute.

Back in the early and mid-80's, DNA had not yet become a fixture in criminal investigations. It was still encumbered by the need for rather large amounts of sample testing material. If large samples could be obtained, DNA was considered the last word, an unquestioned tool that could match a criminal to the genetic material he had left behind at the crime scene. Or, in the cases of the innocent, eliminate the possibility of guilt by identifying someone else.

In the late 1980's, most death row cases had not gone through DNA testing, usually because there weren't enough cell samples for reliable results. Throughout the 1990's, increasingly sensitive instruments allowed laboratories to get DNA readings from smaller and smaller amounts of genetic material left on or inside a victim. It worked in old cases as well as new. If the original evidence in an old case had been saved, the DNA could be read many years later and compared to the person who had been convicted of the crime.

Slowly, the science of DNA permeated the legal system. That's when the cracks in the system became visible. As DNA became the ultimate test of guilt or innocence, it also became the ultimate measure of the legal system itself. And that judgment would not be good. The entry hole blown open by DNA would reveal a system awash in flaws, a system so institutionalized it had lost sight of the end goal, justice.

New studies of the legal system contributed to a rising tide of concern across the United States. Professor James Liebman of Columbia University School of Law studied twenty-three years of capital cases and found reversible error in seven of every ten capital sentences. He found so many mistakes, he concluded there are "grave doubts whether we do catch them all." When Professor Liebman looked at Illinois, he found the overall rate of serious error in capital sentences to be 66 percent, slightly lower than the national average of 68 percent. Professor Liebman concluded that "flaws in America's death-penalty system have reached crisis proportions."*

---

*James Liebman, *A Broken System: Error Rates in Capital Cases, 1973–1995.*

The Center on Wrongful Convictions at Northwestern University School of Law came to the same conclusion. The center is a leader among a loose network of lawyers who donate their time and talents to correcting death penalty mistakes. These lawyers recognize that there are inevitably too many errors within the justice system to use it as a basis for taking a human life. Theirs is a battle against judges who don't want their judgments questioned; against prosecutors and defense lawyers who made mistakes; against shoddy investigators; and against a criminal justice system that tends to hide from criticism.

When Governor Ryan asked how thirteen innocent men could wind up on death row, the Northwestern Center opened its bulging files to highlight eight primary reasons why the system routinely breaks down. The Center noted:

- Defense lawyers who were inexperienced were handling capital cases. Often underpaid, these lawyers did not provide a vigorous defense as required by their profession, resulting in ineffective representation.
- Prosecutors who in their zeal to win a case suppressed, manipulated, or lied about evidence which might have helped the defendant but in so

doing would have hurt their own case. Knowing their career path depended on winning convictions, and driven by their desire to defend the public and achieve success for themselves, they did a disservice to justice.

- Bad science that produces bad evidence. Until the mid-1990's, DNA testing was often unreliable. Now the testing itself is more reliable, but the results are too easily tampered with. Collusion between prosecutors and some laboratories has resulted in doctored evidence intended to slant juries' decisions.

- Unreliable eyewitnesses who are even less reliable when police fail to follow professional guidelines in presenting lineups.

- Jailhouse informants who are often promised good treatment or leniency in their own sentences in exchange for testimony that will help the prosecution. The inducement to get out of jail is too great to expect a convicted criminal not to tell a prosecutor what he wants to hear.

- Bad judges who show bias against a defendant and have steered juries toward convictions.

- Coerced confessions that are obtained by disreputable police interrogation techniques.

- Circumstantial evidence that allows a series of

16   I N T R O D U C T I O N

assumptions to be made from fragments of evidence.*

On April 15, 2002, Governor Ryan's Commission on Capital Punishment reported its findings after twenty-four months of study. The commission presented eighty-five recommendations to improve the system, but it expressed doubt that any improvements would guarantee that an innocent person would not be executed at some time.

It was nine months later, on January 11, 2003, when Governor George Ryan announced the final decision in his three-year odyssey, commuting the death sentences of 164 Illinois inmates to life in prison without parole. Congratulations were sent by Nelson Mandela and Pope John Paul II.

George Ryan's conversion did not exactly descend in a flash of light. For three years he had struggled with the fact that thirteen innocent men had been sent to death row. He was forced to face the problem because as governor he couldn't get away from it. His official act of appointing the blue-ribbon commission of lawyers was predictable and would have relieved him of the full

* The Center on Wrongful Convictions

responsibility of having innocent people on death row, but he couldn't escape the specter of executing an innocent person or the shock when his faith in the system was shattered. Like most laymen, he had believed deeply in the system without really knowing how it worked. He had an abiding faith that justice prevails in trials, that after the turbulent give-and-take of the courtroom and the histrionics of the trial lawyers, somehow truth emerged. To learn otherwise ripped into his physical constitution like a cancer. The foundation of his beliefs had been shaken. Now he was driven by the born-again faith that comes to a reformer.

Governor Ryan's conversion interested me because I had similar feelings when I first heard about the "lucky 13." It was a visceral feeling down inside where instinct comes from. There were no fireworks to mark the moment, no flashes of light. But I knew that the thirteen exonerated men would shadow me. I couldn't shake them loose. They opened all kinds of questions: Was the DNA revolution revealing more than mistakes in a few trials? Was it exposing massive cracks in our legal system?

In answering those questions, I knew I would face a bigger problem. I was biased on two counts. First, I thought some people deserved to die for their crimes. For most of my life I had supported capital punishment. I viewed prosecutors and their police investigators as the thin blue line between good and evil, our best hope for achieving true community. And second, as a lawyer, I had a deep faith in our system of justice. I had attended Washburn University School of Law in Topeka, Kansas, where, as in most law schools, students are taught the law as it *should* be practiced. Reality comes from the partner who tells you how it really *is* practiced.

In 1966, upon graduation, I was excited to pass the bar exam and get down to the business of trial work when something unusual blew me off course. I had worked at WIBW-TV through law school as an announcer, weatherman, and finally part-time anchor. On June 8, I took some time from my bar review course to fill in for the news director who wanted to get started on his vacation a day early. Shortly after the 6:00 evening news a weather bulletin warned of severe weather headed toward Topeka. Within a half hour a tornado was slicing its way through the heart of the Kansas state capital. Within twelve minutes, shopping malls, houses, and beautiful sandstone buildings on the Washburn University campus were rubble.

I was the man on camera giving the warning, and the experience changed my life. My legal career was over before it began, and, much like Dorothy in *The Wizard of Oz*, I was blown away from my home in Kansas, toward a thirty-year career with CBS Television and another fifteen years with A&E Television Network.

At both places, I was able to use my legal education. First came a series of high-profile trials for CBS News, including the Chicago Seven trial in 1969 in which seven well-known anti-war protestors were charged with a new federal law that made it a felony to cross state lines to incite a riot. If ever a trial turned into theater, this was it. At least the death penalty was not involved.

I also covered the trial of Charles Manson in Los Angeles in 1970, which became America's horror story. Manson and his three acolytes were accused of killing Sharon Tate, the eight-months-pregnant wife of movie director Roman Polanski, as well as three house guests. Although Manson did not participate in the actual killings, he had masterminded the whole affair, using drugs, sex, and mind control to turn these young people into zombie-like slaughterers. Like most people, I applauded the death penalty for Manson. That sentence was overturned in 1972, when the Supreme Court called the death penalty cruel and unusual punishment in *Furman v. Georgia*. I was disappointed.

I covered other ugly trials. Richard Speck was a petty criminal who worked in the merchant marines when he docked in Chicago and spent the day with a bottle of cheap wine in the blue-collar neighborhood of East Chicago. Someone told him of a possible score in a townhouse full of student nurses. He slipped in through a screened window and waited as they came home from work. One by one over a seven-hour period, he knifed and strangled seven young women. When police arrived to investigate they had to put a wooden plank across the floor so they wouldn't lose their footing in inch-thick blood. I was present outside the Peoria, Illinois, courtroom when prosecutor Bill Martin announced the death penalty leveled against Speck and was again disappointed when the *Furman* decision later saved his life.

Spared execution and even a jail term on death row, Speck pushed a cart down the corridors of various Illinois maximum security prisons such as Stateville Correctional Facility near Joliet, where he painted the walls, over and over. In an infuriating revelation in 1991, I received a videotape showing Speck and his homosexual lover in prison having sex, snorting cocaine and playing with a pile of hundred dollar bills. It was taped in a room where Speck and his friends operated with a shocking casualness without fear of being interrupted. After we aired several reports using the video, authorities initiated four concurrent investigations, which resulted in major changes within the Illinois correctional system. Speck died of a heart attack in 1991.

John Wayne Gacy was another who I believed deserved to die. He had seduced more than twenty young men off the streets of Chicago for homosexual acts after which he would strangle and bury them under his suburban home.

Through these cases, I learned there is true evil in the world, personified by predators who prey on the unsuspecting. They were my personal combat experience, and they would have hardened any observer. How then could I change my mind?

There is only one thing that would overturn my desire to rid the world of such monsters and that is the fear of convicting and executing an innocent person. When the thirteenth exoneration was announced from Illinois' death row I was shaken in the same way as George Ryan. The Greek term is *peripeteia,* that moment when you realize that all you have believed is wrong.

If these death row verdicts were wrong, how reliable was the system? Were the tools that we had been taught to believe were finely tuned to produce the truth, the whole truth and nothing but the truth actually producing nothing of the sort? The ramifications were almost too frightening to consider. I found lawyers and police friends avoiding the subject as if the legal establishment was pulling a blanket of silence over the matter. For

young attorneys there was too much career risk in
becoming a whistleblower.

My first thought was that better legal minds than
mine should be studying the problem. Then I found out
that small groups of lawyers had been researching and
writing papers for years with no appreciable change. My
own epiphany came when I ran into a dissenting opinion Supreme Court Justice Thurgood Marshall had
written in 1976. In *Gregg v. Georgia,* which allowed state
legislatures to reinstate the death penalty if they provided proper guidelines, Marshall wrote: "In Furman,
the American people are largely unaware of the information critical to a judgment on the morality of the
death penalty . . . if they were better informed, they
would consider it shocking, unjust, and unacceptable."

I kept asking myself, "Unaware of what information?"

Justice Marshall clearly believed that if the American
people knew the real workings of the system they would
be against the death penalty. I wondered: If they were
properly informed, would reasonable people conclude
that our criminal justice system has too many working
parts and requires too many subjective decisions to be
the foolproof machinery needed to make decisions of
death?

Informing people is what my life has been about. So
I embarked on a reporter's journey. I would revisit two

death penalty cases in which the convicted men were later exonerated. I would go back over the crime, the investigation, the trial, the sentence, the appeal, and the exoneration to try to detect exactly where the system went wrong.

First I had to pick my cases. I wanted two cases where, on the surface, everything should have worked perfectly; where both teams of counsel were talented and responsible; where the judge was of good reputation; and where the law enforcement officers gathered evidence to support the prosecution without obvious coercion. In short, I looked for typical American trials, the kind that happen in one form or another in every jurisdiction in the United States. There was one exception: The penalty of death was on the table.

I settled on two cases: Ray Krone and Thomas Kimbell. Both cases come from jurisdictions beyond the major metropolitan areas where overcrowded dockets create their own unique set of problems. And in both cases, the accused were white and middle-class. Race and poverty are major factors in why the death penalty is not applied fairly throughout the United States. I wanted to move beyond those points to other failings of the system just as egregious, but not as well documented.

George Ryan's plea became my mantra: What went

wrong? I felt the answer to the governor's question was deep inside the trials, in the nuances of testimony, the performances of individual lawyers, and the tactical choices made in the heat of a trial. It was somewhere beyond the area of judicial review, where only the most flagrant errors of procedure are heard. In each case, I found a complicated system operated by human beings trying valiantly to reach the most important decision one can ever face—to take someone's life. That task should require a perfect, unassailable system.

I came to the conclusion that such a system is impossible.

PART 1

Case 1: Ray Krone

Our system of criminal justice does not work with the efficiency of a machine—errors are made and innocent as well as guilty people are sometimes punished.

JUSTICE WILLIAM O. DOUGLAS,
FURMAN V. GEORGIA, 1972

CHAPTER 1

From the Crime to the Trial

The CBS Restaurant and Lounge in Phoenix, Arizona, is the perfect spot for guys who want to check out of life for a few hours. Its bland, off-white exterior stucco sandwiched between brick columns makes it indistinguishable from its more reputable neighbors.

Lounges like the CBS are surrogate homes for singles, divorcees, drifters, and floaters, seeking a friendly face, a cold beer, and if the stars align properly, a sexual encounter. It doesn't take much—a loose tank top, tight jeans, and a quick smile will do it for some men. For others, eye contact held a second too long or the brush of the bartender's fingers when she gives back change for a twenty.

Kim Ancona was the attractive manager of the CBS Lounge. At thirty-six, she was not quite as trim as a jogger, but her light brown hair fell just above her shoulders in the casual yet fashionable style of young women who work to keep their appearance up. For Kim, looking good was all part of the job. And she needed a job. She was a divorced mother of three, ages eighteen, fourteen, and ten. She lived with a man named Paul Clark but was thinking of ending the relationship.

Kim looked older when the harsh Phoenix sun exposed thin wrinkles on her face, but in the dim, flattering light of the CBS Lounge she became every girlfriend the male customers could ever remember. And that's one reason the owner, Hank Arredondo, gave her the manager's job.

On Saturday night, December 28th, 1991, Kim Ancona was working her first night as bar manager, and she planned to close around 2:00 A.M. Closing was a matter of wiping down the bar and sliding the stools under the tables so the next day's shift could start fresh. The soda stock needed to be replenished and the compressed-air dispensers for colas and mixers filled. The floors had to be mopped.

Inside, the CBS Lounge was larger than its shopping mall front suggested. A high ceiling fan spread cooled air over some two dozen round tables. Black plastic ash trays and menus stuck in metal holders sat in the middle of each table. Big-screen television monitors and glowing advertisements for beer and liquor brightened the walls.

Bottles of liquor stood on a mirrored counter behind the bar. Kim kept the lights low. From behind the bar, a customer could be hard to identify and hard to remember if he sat with his back to the bar.

Three nights earlier, on Christmas night, Kim had helped Patricia Chipley close up. They were two of three young women who kept the place going and had developed a closeness born of a common labor. The CBS had become their second home.

After closing, Ray Krone, a patron who lived nearby and frequented the CBS, took Kim to the Library Lounge and then to Patricia's home, where they hung out until the early morning hours of the 26th. One way to avoid Christmas memories is to fight off the dawn with fellow travelers.

Kim had mentioned to her friends that she was attracted to Ray, and he may have felt the same. He got into a fight one night at the CBS Lounge with another man who was flirting with Kim. But the relationship had not yet matured beyond a few dates.

Two nights later, another barmaid named Kay Koeste offered to help Kim close up on Saturday night, but she declined, saying "Ray" was going to show up and help.

Beyond these comments the trail goes quiet about what happened that early Sunday morning, December 28th. The factual hole lasts seven hours until 8:10 A.M., when Hank Arredondo arrived to meet a repairman. He found the front door unlocked and the lights still on, a strange oversight for a brand-new manager who'd been so excited to get the job. He checked the bar and noticed nothing wrong.

Then he got to the men's bathroom. He saw the naked body of a young woman sprawled on her back with her head lodged in a corner and her legs stretching past the urinal toward a blue toilet stall. He recognized his manager, Kim Ancona. She looked much younger than her thirty-six years as she lay splayed out, bare limbs against the cold tile floor. Her jeans and her black tank top had been ripped off. Her panties had been cut off and thrown under the urinal. Only her black socks remained on. A thick mass of clotted blood was wrapped like a necklace around her neck. Some dark blood spots dotted the tile floor, but relatively little blood spatter could be seen on the walls.

Arredondo called 911.

Eleven days later on January 8, 1992, Phoenix homicide detective Chuck Gregory told a grand jury that Kim had received six stab wounds, which formed the ring circling her neck. It was not a classic throat cutting, but wounds of direct insertion, which accounted for the lack of blood on the walls. These jabs were not what killed her. A final knife wound on the left side of her back was the entry point for the deathblow, which punctured and collapsed her lung.

Phoenix police cordoned off the scene so Gregory's team could work. They quickly found the kill weapon, a boning knife, underneath a plastic bag that had been placed in the trash can in the bathroom. There were several paper towels in the bag hiding the knife. Did the killer wash his hands and clean the scene before leaving? Did he linger over the body to appreciate his work? Was this an impulse killing or a carefully planned murder?

Gregory checked with the kitchen, and, according to the cook, a knife was missing, the knife in question. He pointed out something significant: The knife was bent, probably not from the soft tissue of the neck. It must have bounced off a rib in that final thrust to the lung.

The police took fifty fingerprints from the crime scene, but none matched the eventual suspect. A small amount of semen found inside the victim was traced to a third person. All of the blood at the scene, on the floor, the knife, and the neck belonged to Kim Ancona. The saliva swabs from her body surface all came up a common blood type, type O.

In 1991, DNA tests were not common usage because

large samples were needed for testing. But the saliva was preserved from Kim Ancona's pubic area and from around the nipple on her left breast. There was a deep bite mark with both upper and lower teeth impressions left in a circle around the entire areola, the area of pigmented skin around the nipple. It had been made postmortem, after her death. The tank top she was wearing might have soaked up some of the saliva. But none could be seen with the naked eye.

Kim's vagina walls were torn. It would later be argued the lacerations were made not from a penis but a broken stick, which had apparently been used to prop the bathroom door open. The stick was found nearby with Kim's blood on its jagged edges.

A few hairs were found on her stomach.

Some detectives thought they had a necrophiliac on their hands, perhaps a sexual predator, who liked to leave behind the savage evidence of his work.

Kim Ancona's murder was the kind of ruthless act that sends a surge of adrenalin through police departments. The image of a young woman discarded like a used paper towel doesn't leave the mind for a long time. Gregory's team wanted to find the killer, and soon.

The community, stunned by the heinous crime, also

clamored for a quick resolution. Authorities pressed for an arrest as soon as possible, which sent police looking for fast leads. And Kim's elderly mother provided an emotional call for vengeance. How could anyone do this to her daughter? All signs seemed to point to a sexual sadist.

Perhaps the most common fault with criminal investigations is their failure to explore all the possible suspects. When attention begins to focus on a single individual, too often the detectives are called off the general hunt to go after the single target. Tunnel vision sets in.

That's what happened in the case of Kim Ancona. Within hours, detectives found a suspect who seemed to fit their bill so well that they felt there was no need to pursue other leads. They had their man. The search was virtually shut down so investigators could concentrate on gathering evidence for trial. None stopped to ask, Do we have the right man?

It wasn't hard to find someone to blame for the murder. A man named "Ray" lived nearby. His name was found in Kim Ancona's address book and he was said to have dated her. Remember, Kim had told Kay Koeste that "Ray" was going to help her close on Saturday night.

But when Detective Gregory interviewed Ray Krone

in the doorway of his home around 2:00 P.M. the day of the murder, Krone had an alibi. He said that he had gone to bed at 10:00 P.M. on Saturday night and slept through till Sunday morning.

But he also seemed rather nervous. At first he denied that he had been seeing Kim. But as they rode to the Phoenix police station Ray told Gregory he, in fact, *had* been with Kim at times outside the CBS Lounge. When Gregory pointed out that was in conflict with his earlier statement, Ray said he didn't mean he had *never* been with her only that he was not her boyfriend.

Krone's roommate confirmed that Krone had been home when he (the roommate) went to bed at 11:30 P.M. and when he got up the next morning Krone was still at the house. Of course, since he didn't sleep in the same bed with Krone he couldn't know if Ray had left and come back during the night.

A neighbor told the detective that he had noticed something out of the ordinary. Ray Krone drove a '74 Chevy Corvette and parked it on a common driveway, a concrete slab that connects both residences. The neighbor said that Krone always covered the car up for the night. It was that kind of car, one you treat like an expensive poodle by tucking it in for the night. But that Saturday night, December 28, the cover was not on the car, and when the neighbor woke up the next morning, it was still not on the car. Did it mean Ray Krone had driven it back to the CBS Lounge to kill Kim Ancona and then return to his bed before his roommate awoke in the morning?

That was good enough for Deputy County Attorney Noel Levy. Levy didn't have to prove guilt beyond a reasonable doubt in his presentation before the grand jury, only that there was probable cause for a murder indictment. Ray Krone could have left his house after his roommate went to bed, murdered Kim Ancona, and returned to bed before his roommate got up in the morning. "Except," said the prosecutor, "he made one mistake. He forgot to cover his Corvette."

Before the grand jury, Levy and his associate Kathleen Bayley presented a shovelful of facts that, standing alone, appeared insignificant but, placed together in a linear narrative in court, seemed to lay a path toward one conclusion: Ray Krone should be charged with the sexual assault and murder of Kim Ancona.

The case hinged on one crucial piece of evidence, which would sway the Maricopa County grand jury and other juries to follow. The impression on Kim's skin left by the teeth that bit her nipple after she was killed was quite clear in its detail. The two front teeth were crooked. The left of the two turned inward at a sharp angle, which formed a pattern that was distinct and could be easily identified. When Detective Gregory talked with Ray Krone he could see that Ray's two front teeth also were crooked. When the detective asked about his teeth, Ray said he'd been involved in a head-on car accident and his face had struck the dash breaking his jaw. That's why his teeth were crooked.

On the way downtown for further questioning, the detective asked Krone to bite into a Styrofoam cup so that he could match the impression of Ray's teeth against the marks on Kim Ancona's breast. Phoenix police forensic scientist Dr. John Piakis had a cast made of Ray's impressions just two days after the murder. When the dental cast was taken to the County Morgue and placed directly over the bite marks around Kim Ancona's nipple, Gregory told the grand jury, they "looked perfect." Further, he said, "Dr. Piakis says that everything was consistent and there was no inconsistencies found in the teeth marks compared to Ray's teeth." On January 28, 1992, Dr. Piakis confirmed his analysis in a letter to Detective Gregory, saying, "it is highly probable that the dentition of Ray Krone caused the bite mark on the left breast of Kim Ancona."

This made matters much worse for Ray Krone. The bite around the nipple after death was so cruel and heinous it was assumed to be the work of a depraved mind and qualified as an aggravating factor, which made Ray eligible for the death penalty in Arizona.

The grand jury returned true bill 141st grand jury 87, a capital offense under A.R.S. 13-3961, and officially indicted Ray Krone for Kim Ancona's murder.

Things didn't look good for Krone. The bite mark match seemed to be absolute proof of his guilt. It was supported by the kind of circumstantial tale a jury is all too ready to buy in the case of an attractive young life destroyed in such a horrifying manner.

The system was lining up against Ray Krone. So was public opinion. The community felt safer with him arrested. The prosecutors filled the media with just enough choice tidbits of evidence to sway the minds of the public. They believed in Ray's guilt. The prosecutors felt confident with their evidence. The police looked like geniuses with their quick investigative work. No one seemed to notice that Ray Krone didn't match the profile of a depraved sexual sadist who could leave a woman spread-eagled on a bathroom floor.

Ray Krone didn't look like a beast. And he didn't act like one, either. His history didn't indicate a Jekyll-and-Hyde personality that would unleash the kind of fury necessary to commit the crime for which he was indicted.

Krone would later write in the Op-Ed page of the *Milwaukee Journal Sentinel:*

I grew up in York, Pennsylvania, with a loving family and many friends. I played Little League baseball, went hiking with the Cub Scouts and Boy Scouts, attended Sunday school and sang in the church choir. I graduated in the top 10% of my high school class and did well on my college entrance exams. I decided to enlist in the Air Force, where I proudly attained the rank of sergeant. I served my country for seven years and was honorably discharged. My last assignment in the Air Force was in Arizona. I decided to stay there and join the U.S. Postal Service. I had a normal, good life.

This was all true. Thin and tall, Ray could have been a dead ringer for, well, an ex-military postal worker. In short, he was a responsible, straight-up, educated, thirty-four-year-old white American male. One sure indicator of his character, the little old ladies along his route would give him pies at Thanksgiving and Christmas. They couldn't believe he would be involved with something like this. But they were among the few.

As for Ray Krone, he believed in the criminal justice system with the blind faith of most law-abiding citizens who spend their lives on the periphery never having to look in. Krone also supported the death penalty. But now that he was in the grips of the Arizona criminal justice system, he wasn't feeling quite so confident. Still, he told himself, he was innocent, so everything had to work out all right.

Ray's first trial was scheduled for April 2, 1992, three months after his arrest. But it was postponed until the fall, as is par for the course, for a variety of legal motions. Once it got underway, the trial lasted seven days, for which Ray's lawyer, Phoenix defense attorney Jeffrey Jones, was paid roughly $5,000. If that sounds like a handsome sum—more than $700 a day—consider the time Jones was supposed to have spent researching and preparing to defend his client's life. Suddenly the pay—$35 an hour—doesn't look so good.

And consider the inequity Jones faced. He was a one-man show, while the prosecutor had the entire Phoenix Police Department, the Maricopa Crime Lab, a full staff, and a co-prosecutor at his disposal. While Jones got $5,000 for his services, the county would pay its key witness, a forensic bite mark expert, more than $50,000 for his testimony alone.

But let's not leave the impression the defense lawyer can't avail himself of similar resources. He can ask for tests and petition the court for money to pay for his own experts to refute the testimony of the prosecution's witnesses.

Defense attorney Jones made such a motion on March 3, 1992, in preparation for trial. He knew the key evidence against his client was the bite mark match. He also knew he was going to have to hire his own expert witness on bite marks to help him interview the prosecution's expert witness, Dr. Raymond Rawson, a flamboyant Nevada state senator as well as an orthodontist and trial expert in bite mark evidence. On paper, Dr. Rawson was impressive. He was also a showman.

Jones didn't know anything about bite mark evidence or any dentists who did. So he hired a friend of his wife's, a dentist named Dr. Bruce Etkin. Dr. Etkin had no qualifications in bite mark testimony. That became clear as soon as the two men flew to Las Vegas to interview Dr. Rawson. Etkin took one look at the opposing expert and said, I can't refute this guy; I don't know anything.

Jones was also impressed by Dr. Rawson. In fact, he was so taken with Dr. Rawson's deposition that he began to doubt his own client. A few days later, he met with Ray Krone, who was anxious to know how things had gone in Las Vegas. Krone was shocked when Jones asked him, in effect, is there any way you could have bitten Kim at some other time? Jones tried to get Ray to come clean and admit that it was his bite. "Look, Ray," Jones said, "the bite's yours." Jones was using a common approach by lawyers who are turned by the opposition's evidence. He was trying to get his client to face reality so they could properly plead and bargain for the least punishment. But Ray declined, offering to take a polygraph to convince Jones he wasn't lying. The polygraph turned out to be inconclusive.

Jeffrey Jones was left without a bite mark expert. Still, he thought he would at least be able to keep his client off death row. After all, Ray's DNA had not been found at the scene, he had a good alibi, and there was no other solid evidence like fingerprints or a confession that tied him to the crime.

Jones was wrong. He didn't understand how strong forensic evidence and its compelling presentation by Dr. Rawson could be. He underestimated the overwhelming effect of the prosecution's case. Jones was not prepared, especially for Rawson's secret weapon, which turned up less than a week before trial.

Dr. Rawson had prepared a video labeled "Bite Mark Evidence Ray Krone." The prosecution presented it to defense counsel on Friday, July 24th. Jones wasn't able to watch it until Sunday, July 26th, the day before trial. The tape was a blockbuster, well produced and drop-dead impressive. It showed a match between Krone's teeth and the bite marks on Kim Ancona's body by overlaying one image on top of the other. It took the dental casts, the Styrofoam impressions, and even CAT scans that the doctor had prepared and overlaid them on the actual wounds. The impact was explosive. The videotape presented evidence in ways that would have been impossible using static exhibits.

Jones was caught off guard. Here was evidence that had not been available during discovery, the period prior to trial in which both sides are required to put their evidence on the table to avoid surprises and limit a trial to more important issues. In this case, the videotape came too late to allow Jones to adequately prepare by making his own tape, finding an expert to rebut Rawson, or even being able to study the tape thoroughly. When confronted, the prosecution claimed even it had not received the tape until July 24th, but it wanted to use the tape nevertheless.

On Monday, Jones moved to preclude the videotape on grounds that it was submitted too late, that he had too little time to answer it, and that it would give an unfair advantage to the prosecution. The motion was taken under advisement. One week into the trial the prosecution asked the court again to admit the tape for Rawson's appearance. This time, the judge allowed it.

The tape was Ray Krone's downfall. Dr. Rawson used it like Ron Popeil demonstrating a new carrot dicer. He performed magnificently and effectively. No other evidence would be necessary. The video did it for the jury.

Jones must have known it. He tried valiantly to attack the tape. On Thursday, August 6th, just before he rested the defense case, he asked to be granted a one-month recess to allow his own expert to produce a tape or, at least, give him time to discredit Dr. Rawson by finding other trials in which he had testified, on the chance he had been wrong. Both motions were denied.

A few days later the jury foreman gave the verdict: "Guilty of murder in the first degree."

Ray Krone had been convicted of first-degree murder and kidnapping but acquitted of sexual assault. He found it ironic that the prosecution's case had been based on sexual assault as the motive, yet he was found innocent of that charge.

He remembers his reaction vividly. It was disbelief:

Now I'm in a whirl. It's like I mean I, I can't believe they found me guilty. I didn't do this. How can I be guilty of something I didn't do? How can that be our justice system? But then again it's like well, you got acquitted of sexual assault, how can that—I mean I was in a little bit of turmoil, as far as understanding how, how did this all happen and what just happened and where did this come from?

I mean, I was shocked of course by, by the guilty verdict but if you could be shocked and not surprised, I don't know if that's possible.

The courtroom erupted in applause and cheers. Kim Ancona's mother hugged and congratulated the prosecution.

Then came the sentencing. Citing one aggravating factor, murder committed in a heinous or depraved manner, Jeffrey A. Hotham, judge of the Superior Court of Arizona in Maricopa County sentenced Ray Krone to death. That one aggravating factor was the bite on Kim's breast.

How does Ray remember this announcement?

I wasn't surprised when I was sentenced to death. The judge never ruled in our favor on anything. I wasn't startled, I wasn't stunned, and I honestly didn't recognize what the consequences really meant. I mean, that's just the same to me as, I'm away from my family, my friends and no longer have a life. That's all it meant. It's just a continuation of this whole nightmare. Death row, jail, prison, I mean it didn't matter. I mean, I never been to death row so what did I know? It didn't matter to me. I'm still removed from my life. I'm treated now as an animal. I'm no longer part of society. I've been isolated and, so death penalty, I mean, unless they just walked up and shot me right there, I mean it was numb, it was surreal, it didn't matter what the heck the judge said.

Jeffrey Jones was reportedly shattered after the trial. He was a former prosecutor and a very capable attorney. His decision to open a private practice and obtain a contract to defend indigent people in the county had certainly not been motivated by a desire to get rich. He wanted to help people. The last thing he thought would happen was a death penalty for Ray Krone. He knew the judge when he had been a county prosecutor. He was also an old friend of the chief prosecutor, Noel Levy. Because he had worked with them both, he thought they would at least not let Ray Krone die. But the dynamics of the Phoenix criminal justice system were against him.

Krone remembers the actual moment vividly:

You're told not to show any emotion; you're told not to look at the jury; your attorney tells you all these things you're supposed to do. And so you're—you almost kind of like sit there and freeze 'cause, I mean you realize the importance of what you're going through, but, but then again you also think just get this over with 'cause the right thing is gonna happen and everything will work out.

But in Ray's case, everything did not work out. The state wanted to take his life.

Ray continues: "And you wonder, why are they doing this? What's, you know, what's going on? And you almost got the feeling that this isn't any attempt to get at the truth. This is an attempt to paint a picture that's abstract and not real."

Abstract. Not real. That's a good description of what a prosecutor does. A prosecutor has to paint a picture of what he *thinks* happened. It's as if he is connecting dots of evidence to re-create the truth. How many cases hinge on a prosecutor's vision of what the pieces of evidence mean? In Ray's case, one of those pieces was a hearsay comment that Ray was going to help Kim close the bar. But which Ray? Was there another Ray who frequented the bar? The Corvette was not covered. Did that prove Ray had left and come back after killing Kim Ancona? And what physical evidence pointed to his guilt? No fingerprint or DNA swab could place him at the scene, only the bite mark testimony, which would later prove to be faulty. And what about Ray's alibi? Hadn't a witness, Ray's roommate, confirmed that he had been at home the night of the murder?

Here's how Ray Krone sees it:

And I'm sitting here saying to myself, am I the only one in here knows the truth? I had a roommate that stayed at my house at the time that knows I never left the house and they had the nerve when he got up there on the stand and talked and told them what happened, the prosecutor got up there to cross-examine him. The prosecutor looked at him for a little bit, he said, "You've known Ray Krone a long time, haven't you?" At that time I'd known Steve for about, about twelve years and my friend Steve said, "Yes, I have." And the prosecutor said, "And Ray Krone's always been there helping you out, being there as a good friend to support you and help you any time you needed him, hasn't he?" And of course, again, Steve said, "Yes, he has, absolutely." "And you'd lie for him wouldn't you?" and [then the prosecutor] turned and walked away. That's what the prosecutor did, that's how he cross-examined my friend, a guy that's just a straight-up regular citizen, took an oath to tell the truth, and that's how he was treated by the prosecutor.

That's exactly how a talented trial lawyer handles an opposing witness. Levy's dramatic cross-examination destroyed Ray's alibi. What was the jury supposed to do? It was faced with a difficult choice, the integrity of the witness against the possibility raised by the prosecutor that that witness would lie for a friend.

Let's say the jury couldn't make up its mind. So they turned to the rest of the evidence in the prosecution's case to tip the scales, reasoning that because they believed the bite mark evidence, everything else had to support it. Therefore, the friend must have been lying. It is a dramatic example of why bad evidence admitted improperly can do such damage.

That's the way the system works, perhaps the only way it can work. But the odds are still only 50-50 that the jury's judgment will be the truth. Sometimes the truth prevails when the jury sees a lawyer put things in perspective. This time, it did *not* lead to the truth. Ray Krone was innocent. But nothing could counteract the bite mark testimony. It was too powerful. Once the discovery rule was violated, the defense never caught up, never figured out how to explain the seemingly unassailable expert testimony and videotape. The videotape became the prosecution's strongest piece of evidence and Noel Levy used it effectively to win a guilty verdict. Only Ray's defense lawyer had the opportunity to stop the relentless movement toward a guilty verdict, but he was outsmarted and outmaneuvered and lost a death penalty case in the process.

The prosecutor's case was circumstantial, a picture of what *might* have happened based on the circumstances of the crime. Levy pieced together isolated events and tidbits of evidence and wove them into a compelling story. According to the dictionary, circumstantial evidence points "indirectly to a person's guilt but not conclusively proving it." Without circumstantial evidence, many guilty criminals would go free. However, death penalty cases should not hinge on circumstantial evidence. There is too high a risk that the wrong version of events will be sold by a persuasive prosecutor. That's what happened in Ray Krone's case. Part of the problem, as Ray Krone says, is that the prosecutor has the last word: "A lot of times he'll save some of his powerful stuff for that last rebuttal because we get, the defense gets, one chance at cross-examination. The prosecutor gets the final say, so now he can bring on his really powerful ammunition, knowing that the defense can't get up there and say anything about it again."

It's true. In many states, the state delivers the first final arguments, the defense closes, and then the prosecution has the last word with a rebuttal. Unfair? It must seem unfair to an innocent defendant sitting helplessly behind a table, instructed to show no emotion, make no outburst, and not look at the jury. But the state would argue that it has the burden of proving its case beyond a reasonable doubt, which is such an advantage to the defendant that the prosecution requires extra help at the end.

For a number of years, the Ray Krone conviction was known as the perfect case. A young woman, Kim Ancona, was hideously murdered. The outraged and terrified community was quickly appeased with an arrest attributed to good police work. A popular and capable prosecutor overwhelmed the defense with incontrovertible proof of guilt and won a conviction for the community and the victim's grieving family. A jury delivered the appropriate ending with a verdict of guilty followed by a sentence of death. Open. Shut. Life goes on.

After the whirlwind passed, only one man knew the truth, and he was heading for death row.

CHAPTER 2

Life on Death Row

Ray Krone's world had changed with a single word. The criminal justice system, in which he had believed, had declared him guilty of kidnapping and murder and had sentenced him to death. It seemed that he and his family and close friends were the only ones in the world who believed that he had not murdered Kim Ancona. But for now, there was nothing they could do.

After his sentencing, Ray Krone was transported from the Maricopa County Jail in Phoenix to Florence, home of Arizona's death row in November, 1992. He remembers the moment when he was given a jumper suit and bound up in chains before he was led to a van:

"I mean I had chains just about everywhere except across my eyes and my neck. I was chained up and they put me in a van by myself and drove me straight to death row. And I remember walking in the doors, shuffling my feet and dragging in there and it was deathly quiet, and where I just come from, the county jail, it was always loud and noisy."

There's one thing death row inmates get when they are christened with their new status—respect. Other inmates quiet down in their presence. Whether it's out of fear or pity, the guards treat them with special care. Death row inmates do not mix with the general population. That separation gives them a certain celebrity in prison usually enhanced by the publicity of the crime and trial before they arrive.

In the receiving area, Ray Krone changed uniforms and got instructions on how to conduct himself inside the facility. The prison was monochromatic and sterile. It smelled like a hospital with that antiseptic odor of disinfectant everywhere. There were echoes of voices down corridors and the hollow, industrial clanking, the signature of maximum security.

"I was getting the little lecture about, 'I know everything you do in here, you can't get away with nothing, don't do this, you got any tattoos? You belong in a gang? You do this and watch your back' and all this. And I was like, no, no, no, no, no. I don't have tattoos; I didn't belong in any gang. And of course they don't believe that stuff."

What Ray did need to know was protocol, the way to behave in a prison culture under the eyes of guards but under the control of the inmates. "You know, people on death row are tatted out, I mean they're just, you know they got a record a mile long. So it was like, why are you telling me this stuff, I ain't hooking up with no gang. I'm just staying on my own. I went through that lecture thinking, 'Well, that was really, really strange. I mean how does any of that apply to me? What is that, just a scare tactic?'"

It didn't take long for Ray to find out the lecture was not only accurate, but crucial to his survival. "Well, I get put in my cell, it was either the second or the third day I was there and they stabbed my neighbor over a five-dollar debt. A guy came forward and asked him for his money and he made a comment, 'I'll pay you when I feel like it,' or something. Well that's disrespect. Everything in prison is about respect. You know, you gotta be the tough guy, you can't let people walk on you, and you can't let people take advantage of you. And, if a guy even acts like he's disrespecting you, you gotta flair up, you gotta do something about it."

We have to remember that Ray Krone is not a tough

guy. He specialized in electronics in the Air Force, and then delivered mail for the Post Office. He had no criminal record. But in prison he would have to get tough.

Well, anyway, he got stabbed over this five-dollar debt and he didn't scream out, he didn't call out or nothing. He went and laid on his bunk. The reason I know, is 'cause my neighbor, the guy that lived on the one side of me is the one that got stabbed. A man that lived on the other side of me sent me a note and said that something was gonna go down and just ignore it, act like you're asleep. Don't say nothing, just be cool. So now, I'm all nervous. What the heck does he mean, something's going down?

They stabbed the guy. He laid down on his bunk. And eventually enough blood dripped down on the floor so when they did their security walk they found the blood that night and they come in and got him and took him out of there. But see, he never screamed out, he never called out for help, he never did anything 'cause I mean he'd been in prison long enough to know that he got stuck because of his disrespect, 'cause of the words he said.

The stabbing took care of the debt.

Whether it's five dollars or 500 dollars, once you take steel up in you the debt's erased. Unless they were trying to kill you. They might be back for that. But that was just to show him, hey, you don't talk to me like that, you don't treat me like that. It was a respect issue again.

This is the third day I'm there and then it's like I'm thinking this is ridiculous, this guy telling me not to hook up with gangs, not to do drugs, not to get tattoos. I mean third day there and they stab the guy next to me. You find out right away you're not cut off from violence anywhere in prison unless you're isolated by yourself in a room where nobody can ever come in and you never come out. You're never protected. There is no isolation from violence, that's what prison is. The people in there are violent. And so that shocked me early. I kept my mouth shut and I just watched and I tried to find out who were the more respected people there and would talk to them.

Ray Krone's cell was six feet wide and eight feet long. The side that led to the hallway was made entirely of metal plates about two feet wide, with metal bars between them. There was about a two-inch gap between the bars and the plates.

"So you, you actually could look out a little bit. You could stick your arm through that little place. And then you had a metal door, it was all metal, that slid back and forth, and it had an opening in the middle where a tray fit in. It could be closed and locked from the outside. That's where your food tray would come through and other things that were passed into you."

Ray's bunk was fastened on a metal ledge along the wall. Across from it was a little cement table with a cement stool attached underneath. Everything was cement so it couldn't be taken apart and used as a weapon.

"So, basically you could sit on your bed and rest your feet on your table if you laid down. There was a two-foot walkway between your bed and your little two-foot table. And then the back part of your cell was where your sink was, on the top of a commode. It was a one-piece deal where the back part kept extending up higher and there was a sink. So you could sit on the commode and wash your hands at the same time."

Even Krone appreciated the fact that a death row inmate shouldn't expect too many luxuries. A blue plastic tub about a foot deep held everything he possessed. He remembers the cell in such detail because that was his world, a space no bigger than many closets, which he rarely left, except for showers three times a week and an hour's exercise every twenty-three hours.

You weren't allowed much stuff. You could have like five books. You were allowed a TV, which you had to buy. You were allowed a stereo-type boom box. You were allowed a typewriter for legal work. I believe you were allowed one or two photos that you could set up on your table. And you were allowed, I believe it was ten cassette tapes.

You could scrounge stuff up here and there. You keep your plastic spoon off your tray. When the guys would make coffee they would keep a Styrofoam cup whenever they could find it. They sold coffee cups too but some guys didn't have no money, I mean, unless people sent you money.

Prison is a closed society. Very little comes in so those inside create their own rules. Much has been written on the Darwinian nature of prison and its survival of the fittest or the smartest culture. Groups of men band together for protection. A trade network grows. The currency is in commodities, things people want. The more people want something, the higher its value. Cigarettes, magazines, a razor, a towel, a book, drugs. If someone offers you advice, it earns a favor. One third of those in prison can't read or write. So those who can have a service to sell, writing and reading letters from home. This served Ray well.

I'm not the biggest, the baddest, the toughest, the meanest. I don't have that attitude, that mentality. I mean fortunately I'm not physically small and I'm not afraid to defend myself but I'm also not stupid and you can't win if you think taking one guy out is gonna solve the problem, when it turns out that he is hooked up with a gang and you got everybody else to take care of too. I mean you just can't win being an island, so to speak. But you had to have a kind of edge, almost like you had to supply something that they needed.

Well, because of my stupidity, my ignorance of the justice system I realized that the only way I could fight the system is to learn about it and I started to go to the law library and I started reading.

Like I say, I'm more than reasonable intelligence and I could absorb this and I actually could start helping other guys when they needed help with legal stuff. And then I got a job in the law library. There's very few jobs available on death row. They don't let you work. They don't want you to work, but they had to have somebody do it.

Well, now there's a lot of guys that are fighting their legal cases. There are a lot of guys that just need legal help and some of them can't read, some of them can't write. Well, that was my in with the guys that I needed to be in tight with to get some security, to get some safety, to get some protection, so to speak, in prison. I became a legal representative for them and that helped me get through. And I became part of the environment. I felt more secure now, I understood the system more.

Ray Krone had found himself in service to someone else. His price? Security. He adapted and survived.

In prison, 35 cents an hour can make you rich. "The maximum job in prison was 50 cents. So I was very fortunate. Fifty cents an hour, on a 40-hour week. So that was 20 bucks. That's, that was a lot of money in prison. A pack of cigarettes, tobacco and stuff back then was like 60 cents so cigarettes were kind of like cash. Cigarettes and stamps were what we used as cash in there for bets and stuff. You know, I'll bet you a pouch of tobacco or I'll bet you five cigarettes or I'll bet you two stamps, whatever. 'Cause there's gambling goes on. That was our money that we used in prison."

Ray figured out the best way to do hard time, and then he just existed. All choices were taken from him—

when to eat, when to shower, when to go to bed. He became an object in a space where even time is suspended.

"[The cell] is a painted wall, a cement floor that's cold in the wintertime, hot in the summertime. But once you get through those first couple weeks and months, it almost does become home to you. You call it home, you don't say I'm going back to my cell; you say I'm going back to my *house*. You know just little things like that, you start using your terminology. You accept that this is where your life is, this is where you're living now, probably where you'll die if they have their way and it becomes acceptable to you."

In order to escape the numbness of death row, the inmates indulged in their favorite topic of conversation, the last meal.

We'd all talk about what we were gonna have for our last meal. We would plan that.

I actually wanted seafood. You don't get any seafood in there. I actually wanted some scallops. I wanted lima beans, and I wanted a strawberry milkshake.

And every now and then I'd add something to them. I'd say, "Yeah, I want to get some sweet potatoes 'cause I like sweet potatoes." You'd get sweet potatoes twice a year usually. And, so I got to thinking, then I'd say, "Well, I gotta think of something I don't get." And then, I change it. But I basically wanted scallops, shrimp, and lima beans. You didn't get lima beans. I like lima beans.

Oh yeah, Brussels sprouts. I used to go back and forth between Brussels sprouts and lima beans. Then I figure, if I get Brussels sprouts they'd only give me three or four but if I got lima beans they'd give me a bigger spoonful. You know you're just there and you got time to think about crazy stuff like that.

This one guy I know got a carton of cigarettes. He wanted a carton of cigarettes and a six-pack of Coke, that's what he wanted. 'Cause you're put in isolation for I think it's about four days before you get executed. You're taken in to isolation where they can watch so you don't kill yourself, you know, suicide watch. But then you're fed. Well it used to be they executed at one minute after midnight but you were fed around six o'clock that night. So you had like six hours or so to eat your last meal. That's why this guy wanted a carton of cigarettes and a six pack of Coke.

To fill the time.

Certain things stayed with Ray Krone, pieces of the experience that will come back to him when he's least expecting, when a certain sound drifts in on the air or a smell.

> Some of the environment reminds you of a hospital 'cause it's austere, there's no decoration, and everything is just basic plain glass, brick, tile, or whatever. But then of course when you get into the section where the cell blocks are, now you're talking about big metal doors and metal bars with all the windows like a hospital but it's not clean. I mean you have inmates that do the cleaning, but you're given very little in cleaning supplies. They can't give you fancy buckets, mops or any type of caustic cleaning supplies 'cause you know what's gonna happen with it, it's gonna go up against somebody's head or get thrown on them or something.
>
> So you're real limited with what you have to work with so it's not kept very clean and of course when you got, well when I was on death row I believe there was a hundred and—about 110, 112 other inmates in the death row section and these pods were sixteen man. So that's sixteen guys that would use one shower. Some guys didn't use a shower. It was more of a disguised stench.
>
> I mean the guys would spit on the walls. And then things would get spilled or thrown so you could get

sodas, coffee, food up there. If they didn't like the food, they'd throw it back. It would get splattered and it would stay there for a while 'cause inmates would say, "I ain't cleaning that up, you clean it up."

The guards ain't gonna come in here and tell *you* to clean up, and the guards sure ain't gonna clean it up. They don't have private janitors who are gonna clean up. You could see stuff there six months later and you'd go, oh yeah, that's where that so-and-so split that apple up against the wall and tried to hit that guard.

Inmates often kept their own cells clean and tidy, perhaps in order to give themselves a small measure of pride in an otherwise demeaning existence. But public spaces were another matter.

"Anywhere else you went out in the common area, if you went up to the law library and there was a common bathroom there and you had to use it, it was dirty and smelly, you were afraid to sit down on it."

Ray found his senses became more acute.

So the smell became one of the senses that you use. Your ears, of course, were attuned because you had to hear if somebody was coming up behind you. You had to hear if something was happening, if something was going down, you had to hear sometimes what people were talking about. So your ears were definitely sensitive to picking up noises.

It was funny, I just remember my sense of smell. Guys would get a letter in from their girlfriend or wife and you asked them to put perfume on it. Well, then they'd pass it around so all the guys could smell it. Or, some of the magazines you'd get that started doing those scent things years ago when they first started, I mean 'cause that was like something pleasant.

You don't get to smell anything pleasant. And it was such a treat and girls would write me and you could smell the cologne or their perfume on there. I'd put that under the pillow and guys would wrap it up in plastic bags and save it so it wouldn't lose any of its smell. And they'd keep it for months, something that smelled good.

The darkness after lights-out at ten o'clock brought a rare moment of privacy. But even then, Ray had to be prepared for trouble. "Now when it's quiet time and you're lying there on your bunk, your head could be close to the guards. Depending on how you wanna lay, a lot of guys wouldn't lay with their head up near the bars because if somebody wanted to get them it would be too easy to reach through the bars and do it, so they'd put their feet down there. Some of them put their cooler or their TV right up near the bars so the guys couldn't reach in to get at you. People used to put shanks at the end of broomsticks so they could stick it in farther."

Ray Krone was an innocent man sliding toward death in an environment he couldn't control. All that he had worked for was gone. Almost all that he believed in had been destroyed. His days were filled with a single question: Why me? It would have made many stronger men go mad with desperation.

Some death row inmates have spoken about finding Jesus in prison. When all hope is lost, they have found comfort in the New Testament's message that even the worst sinner can be saved. Ray Krone found something else that became his lifeline.

You learn a lot about yourself. If you can be content with nothing in a room the size of a bathroom and still find a way to get through each day and find something to look forward to and something to be thankful for; if you can make the best of that, there's not much worse that can ever happen.

My biggest fear honestly that I had on death row was how I was going to help myself and what this was doing to my family. Those were my fears. I didn't physically fear for myself. I'd already been in fights; I'd already been stabbed. That stuff didn't worry me anymore. Death loses its grip on you, if you don't care if you die. I mean that might solve everybody's problems. It certainly solves your worries anyway.

Once death loses its grip on you, your fear of death, there's almost a peacefulness that can come over you, an existence that's made available. And most of the guys who are on death row have accepted that. They accepted their fate as death and it didn't bother them.

If the public could learn about the stark existence on death row, the mental torture of the isolation, it might very well find satisfaction in the punishment of life in prison without parole.

Despite Ray's newfound calmness, he suffered the mental stress of being alone all the time. The isolation felt like a form of torture:

It wasn't a fear, it was definitely a loneliness thing. There was definitely an isolation thing. There was definitely a communicative, normal physical contact problem.

I don't mean that in any sexual type way, I mean the ability just to shake somebody's hand and greet somebody, say hi to somebody, pat somebody on the back. Any of that type of contact, communication, one-on-one talk, you just couldn't do that there, there was no way to do that. So those little basic things of humanity that we grow up doing in our communicative skills or our coexistence with people was . . . you couldn't even do that there.

I'm an outgoing person, I'm a talkative person, I like interaction with people and now I was a hermit. I didn't talk to people, I did my own things, and I read books and crossword puzzles and kept busy in my own way, to my own self. I would play basketball and I would talk to people and when I was doing my legal help with them I would talk to them. But I found myself withdrawing a lot more and becoming withdrawn was something that I never was.

With each passing year Ray became one of the more experienced hands on the cell block. He would give out advice to younger inmates entering fresh and scared, just as he had arrived.

Young guys come in, they wanna hook up with something. They wanna get affiliated and they wanna get their respect. I was older, I was wiser, I got my respect by my honesty, my integrity and the fact that somebody could come to me and I could help them out if

they needed help and I didn't run my mouth to people. I didn't tell other people's business and so there
was a sense of trust there. And I had a little bit of wisdom, a little bit of knowledge about things that people
could come and ask me questions about and know
that I'd give them the answer if I had it. And that it
wouldn't go any further. A lot of people don't want
you to be talking about their business and they'll tell
you, you keep my name out of your conversation.

Ray explained that it was a privacy issue. When
someone confided in him, he'd make sure it didn't go
any further. He earned their trust which in turn earned
him respect and protection.

"I didn't feel any need to be in prison. I didn't get
any tattoos. That was a medical safety issue right there, I
mean you got guys that are getting tattoos, they're using
the same needle. It's hard to get the equipment but the
ingenuity that they have in prison is amazing. I mean
they probably could've landed a man on the moon
quicker than NASA if they'd just gave them a few little
basic materials, some aluminum foil and a propeller
and I think they could've launched something to the
moon. I mean they are ingenious with the things that
they come up with."

There comes a time, however, when the pressure gets to be too much. And then, even Ray had to take a stand.

I don't react well to pressure. I mean guys start pressuring me I fire back in the other direction. I mean you're not gonna force me to do something I don't wanna do to begin with. I was already an adult. I already knew who I was and what I stood for.

But now you take a youngster coming in straight out of high school or just barely out in life and doesn't know much about himself, he'll fall under anybody's wing and guys will look for kids like that to prey on. I mean they will but it wasn't gonna happen in my case.

Some things in life we learn the hard way and that's something that sticks in our mind and we remember that but you don't wanna be going through prison to learn it the hard way 'cause that can be deadly. I was fortunate that some guys would stop and talk to me, guys that had done time.

I was stabbed in a riot. I was sucker punched more than four or five times, but nobody ever got the best of me. I've been through my share of riots and fights and I still got a scar on my back where eventually a pencil lead worked its way out.

What's the real loss for the wrongfully convicted and incarcerated? For many, the very hardest thing is the pressure of maintaining relations with the outside world, especially the family. Once inside, a man doesn't have any control of the outside. That can play tricks on the mind and make incarceration more difficult.

"I was in prison," Ray Krone continued, "but my family and friends and people who believed in me were doing their own type of time even though they weren't in a physical prison, physical confinement. They had their own type of suffering. If my name came up, if you were a loved one, a sister, a wife, things would have to come up to make you think about where I was.

And I know, they'd tell me how they worried about this. So when you're in there doing time that's one of the things that you'd have to protect. Not only protect yourself but you'd have to protect your family and friends from being hurt and, and being worried about you. And so, you're always trying to tell 'em don't worry. Everything is fine. And you don't let 'em know when you were stabbed or you don't let 'em know when there was a riot, or you try not to or play it down. Because you know that they're worried about you. The people that care about you love you or are thinking about you, are concerned about you, and that's a part that a lot of people don't realize. Most everybody in prison does have somebody that cares about him. At least one. A mom, somebody. Almost everyone.

It was sad for some of the guys in there that they had no family contact, they had nobody to visit 'em. They were the helpless and the hopeless types. And to see somebody lose hope it's really a sad thing in life 'cause I, I didn't. I mean I was a positive person. And that interaction with the people in prison, that had people that cared about 'em on the outside, that you don't realize the emotional strain and struggle that goes by having to interact. Being on the inside you want to maintain that gap, that window to the outside.

But that also involves stress and struggle and turmoil on those people on the outside to allow you that window to be part of their life too. And it's my folks, my friends who could describe it to you. But I just know I felt a real burden to protect them from any of the suffering, any of the dealings that you have to live with in prison. I wanted to protect them from that and they were worried enough as it is without having to know what it was really like. I'm sure a lot of these guys will say to you, try to protect your family and loved ones from knowing what it's really like in there.

The one thing Ray Krone did have was a rabidly loyal family that organized into a pro-active action group. They published newsletters under the title "The Ray Krone Story," which were funded by the Ray Krone Defense Fund. They made sure all the evidence from Ray's trial was on the Internet. They wrote background stories on the defense and prosecution. They were so noisy that on September 11, 1995, Prosecutor Noel J. Levy filed a motion asserting that the newsletter "impeded" the state's right to a fair trial. Judge James McDougall denied Levy's motion.

With close friends fighting on the outside, Ray Krone took heart inside. He couldn't let the team down.

Looking back on his experience, Ray Krone doesn't seem bitter, just resigned to a turn of fate that shortened his life in freedom. But there are specific things he would change in the criminal justice system. He would make it more equitable.

I blame the system for allowing the prosecution unlimited funds and unlimited access to the evidence. I mean who's the first one on the crime? The police department, the prosecution. So how's the defense ever supposed to get access to that evidence unless they get one of those people to turn it over to them?

So they have unlimited access to the crime. [The

prosecution] has all the facilities and the money to pursue a case where the defense doesn't. It's never a balanced field. I say make the law say, whatever is given the prosecution is given to the defense.

Given his hideous experience on death row, you'd think that Ray Krone would consider the death penalty a deterrent to murder. He doesn't. Most criminals don't consider the potential consequences of their actions—they're too caught up in the crime. Plus, he points out that some inmates actually turn down their appeals so they can be executed. They can't bear to continue to live in prison.

A fallacy of the pro–death penalty people is that they think, "Well, that teaches them a lesson, it's a deterrent." It's like, if the guys are volunteering to be executed, how is it a deterrent? You know what I mean? And nobody stops in the middle of a murder to say, "Well, if I'd known I was gonna get the death penalty I'd have never done that." I mean it's no deterrent, it's an act of violence and it's a mental snap. You don't consciously sit there and analyze or contemplate what your penalty is gonna be if you continue in this course of action. I mean it's violence.

While Ray was undergoing his death row transformation, his lawyers were appealing his case to the Arizona Supreme Court. They zeroed in on the bite mark
videotape and its "eve-of-trial" disclosure. Citing Rule
15.1 (a)(3), which requires the state to make available to
the defendant, within ten days of arraignment, the
names and addresses of experts who have personally
examined any evidence, together with the results of
comparisons, they asked the Supreme Court for a new
trial. Chances were good, especially because another
rule requires the state to disclose a list of all papers,
documents, photographs, or tangible objects, which the
prosecutor will use at trial. Clearly, that hadn't happened in Krone's original case.

It was June 22, 1995. Arizona temperatures were
beginning to take the fast climb into the 100s. Ray
Krone had been on death row for three and a half years.

CHAPTER 3

The Appeal

Ray Krone owes a lot to his cousin Jim Rix. One day in 1995, Jim was talking with his mother. "Did you see that TV show last night about the innocent guy in prison?" he asked. And to his great surprise she said, "You have a cousin on death row who's innocent." That just blew Jim Rix away. He had only heard Ray Krone's name two or three times before and he didn't know his cousin was on death row.

Jim Rix had a lucrative computer business selling dentists computer software that helped them run their offices. It meant he could get away from his office without having his business come apart.

Though Jim had never met Ray Krone, the notion of having a cousin in jail for a murder he didn't commit intrigued him. Through a lawyer friend in Phoenix, he obtained the transcripts of Ray's trial. Jim really couldn't tell who was telling the truth from the transcripts. He couldn't tell what might have been wrong. Everything looked good on paper.

Then he decided to take a closer look at the bite mark evidence. He used his contacts in the dental world to track down Dr. Homer Campbell, one of the leading bite mark experts in the country and former president of the American Academy of Forensic Sciences. Campbell was also the chief forensic odontologist at the Office of the Medical Investigator at the University of New Mexico Medical School.

Jim approached Dr. Campbell in between sessions at the annual meeting of the American Academy of Forensic Sciences in San Antonio and asked him to take a look at the bite marks from Ray Krone's trial and render a quick judgment on whether they matched. To his surprise, Dr. Campbell said they did *not* match and that Ray should be excluded as the killer. According to Jim Rix, Dr. Campbell said, "This is bullshit! Who marked this?"

Dr. Campbell agreed to provide an affidavit, which

was included with the appellate arguments in the request for a new trial.

Perhaps never before has a cousin done so much for a relative he had never met.

When Justice Frederick J. Martone concluded the Arizona Supreme Court's decision remanding Ray Krone's case for a new trial, he referred to the late submission of the bite mark videotape, saying, "The State's discovery violation related to critical evidence in the case against the accused. We cannot say it did not affect the verdict."

That's a judicial understatement. The jury had been bowled over by Dr. Rawson's videotape. Just think about it. Audiovisuals have so permeated our lives they have acquired the weight of authority. Advertisers spend millions of dollars creating the most effective visual tricks and stories to get inside our heads and persuade us to purchase specific products. Dr. Rawson's videotape had the same effect. Through visual gimmicks such as instant replay, still-frame overlay, and dissolves, the tape was designed to "deliver the truth" in a compelling, graphic way so that the jurors could easily understand. It managed to convince the jury that Ray

Krone was guilty, obliterating all evidence to the contrary. The jurors were so impressed by the tape that they explained or "conformed" all the rest of the evidence to agree with it. It became the Rosetta stone by which all the other evidence was measured.

Ray Krone's second trial would have a new attorney and new evidence including tests to show that someone else's DNA was present at the crime scene, but would it make any difference? Or would the jury, awed again by Rawson's videotape, explain away all the other evidence?

A noted defense attorney from San Diego, Chris Plourd of the law firm Plourd & Steigerwalt, signed on for the second trial. Plourd was an expert in DNA testing and testimony, a frequent lecturer at forensic science seminars, and an instructor at the American Academy of Forensic Sciences. He immediately began to work on the bite mark evidence, knowing that if he couldn't rebut it, Ray Krone was destined to return to his cell on death row. Plourd's first discovery is a good illustration of why justice is so elusive when filtered through a complex system of rules applied in an adversarial setting where an unexpected piece of evidence might hurt your case.

A prosecutor's career depends on "winning" cases. As a result, prosecutors are often tempted to present only that evidence which supports their argument and to drop that which doesn't, hoping the opposition never finds out about it. And to be fair, the responsibility of the litigators is to make the best case they can for their client, which is hard enough when they're concentrating only on their own side, much less having to do the work of an inadequate opposing counsel. And after all, in an adversarial system, it's the job of the opposing counsel to find his own evidence and make his own case.

But for the court, *justice* is the goal of a trial, not lawyers chalking up wins. The professional dilemma is, how should the system compensate when the trial lawyers are not equally balanced? How can it prevent a talented, ambitious prosecutor from overwhelming a less talented defense attorney?

The criminal justice system does try to rein in the overzealous prosecutor through the use of discovery rules. By opening the files of investigation to both sides, the court eliminates surprises. Both sides can inspect the same evidence and plan their respective cases accordingly. This saves the court time. And any time saved in today's world of crowded dockets is a bonus.

During the initial investigation of Kim Ancona's murder, Dr. John Piakis was the forensic bite mark expert hired by the Phoenix medical examiner to examine the bite mark around Kim's breast. Plourd learned it was only Piakis's third bite mark case. In order to get some training, well before the Kim Ancona murder, Piakis had attended a meeting of the American Academy of Forensic Sciences, where he had met with Dr. Norman Sperber, a nationally recognized bite mark expert from San Diego. Dr. Sperber befriended the young enthusiastic scientist and became Dr. Piakis's mentor.

When Dr. Piakis got the Krone case and took photographs that first night, he immediately sent them along with a report to Dr. Sperber, asking for his guidance. According to Chris Plourd, Dr. Sperber took one look and said, "You've got problems with this. This is not a match."

How did Plourd find this out? It took a bit of sleuthing. Plourd explains: "When I was hired I called up Dr. Piakis and introduced myself, told him where I was from, and he said, 'You know, I think I've heard of you before. Well, you're from San Diego. Do you know Dr. Sperber?'"

"I said, 'Oh yes, very well. Dr. Sperber and I have had cases, you know, on the other side of the fence and I have the utmost respect for him.'"

"Piakis replied, 'Well, he's kind of my mentor and everything.'"

"And I thought," said Plourd, "Why wasn't Dr. Sperber the expert for the prosecution, because that's how things work."

Plourd meant that if Dr. Sperber, the mentor and more established expert, had been helpful to the prosecution, they would have called him as their witness. But clearly Sperber's opinion had been to the contrary— "This is not a match"—so they had dropped him and kept looking for an expert witness who would support their case. That is not unusual. Experts often have different opinions. The defense and prosecution teams each find the expert who agrees with its interpretation of the case and lets the jury decide between them.

But under the rules of discovery, Dr. Sperber's finding was exculpatory evidence—"freed from blame"— and it should have been turned over to the defense even though it would have hurt the prosecution's case. The system is set up to do the right thing, to ensure that justice is produced. Unfortunately, the lawyers don't always follow the rules.

It's easy to understand why the prosecutor would want to drop such a piece of evidence. The thought process might go something like this: "Why should I do the work of the defense attorney? That's what the adversarial system is all about. Let the defense find their own witnesses." But what if the defense attorney is so underpaid or ill-prepared and inexperienced or overloaded with other cases that he fails to find an expert who refutes the prosecution's findings? Should the prosecution sit on its hands during the trial and say nothing, knowing that an expert witness would refute its own evidence?

Who made the decision not to reveal Dr. Sperber's opinion to the Court? Was it Noel Levy, the prosecutor who is famous for controlling all aspects of his cases? Or did Dr. Piakis make the decision not to tell Mr. Levy?

During an interview on August 16, 1994, Chris Plourd tried to get an answer from Dr. Piakis. He asked Dr. Piakis whether he had discussed the case at length with Dr. Sperber. Piakis answered, "You know, I don't remember. I don't remember."

But according to the telephone records of John Piakis from February 16, 1992, he should have remembered. He talked with someone at Dr. Sperber's number in Loma Vista, California, for 81 minutes. It would have been a month and a half after the murder, just when the prosecution team was building its case against Ray Krone.

On the other end of the phone line, Dr. Sperber *did* remember the conversation because he told Chris Plourd that he specifically told the Phoenix forensic odontologist that there was no match.

If we view the incident in a light most favorable to Dr. Piakis, perhaps he was inexperienced and didn't know about things like discovery rules. Or maybe in his zeal to find positive data for the prosecution he failed to tell Mr. Levy about Dr. Sperber's position. To suggest otherwise—that Dr. Piakis told Mr. Levy about Dr. Sperber's exculpatory opinion and that Mr. Levy deliberately kept that opinion from the defense—would be a serious charge and at this point cannot be confirmed. When asked, Noel Levy declined to comment, claiming that making public comment might hinder a related proceeding.

Either way, Ray Krone's first defense attorney, Jeffrey Jones, never heard about Dr. Sperber's opinion and Ray Krone was convicted and sentenced to death without a single suggestion that there was a bite mark expert out there who did not believe the bite was a match. The entire case could have turned around right there—no ten years behind bars for Ray Krone, no three and a half years on death row, no million dollar cost to the taxpayers of Arizona.

Subjective choices and decisions like that happen in one form or another many times in every trial. Most have no bearing on the verdict; they are the mysterious "technicalities" we hear so much about. But some, whether they are innocent, absent-minded moments of forgetfulness or intentional acts of hiding evidence from the other side, can have life-or-death consequences.

Lawyers are human beings who make mistakes. But where death hangs in the balance, we can't afford mistakes.

Back to the bite mark evidence. Plourd studied Rawson's tape closely, reviewing it frame by frame. "When you analyze the video," he told me, "there's actually some manipulation of the images that make it appear it's a match. The key is the distance between the two canines. In Ray's teeth, they're shorter and it's impossible for that to be the bite mark. But in the first video, they actually match up one-to-one. And he [Dr. Rawson] admitted that somehow the images must have been shrunken improperly [to make the match]. It came at the end of his testimony, and I had cross-examined him two or three days. So, the bottom line—I knew what he was pushing wasn't necessarily science. It was sort of a shell-game type thing to get somebody convinced what he was doing was right."

Dr. Rawson did not tell the prosecution how he had prepared the tape. After all, he was the expert, and they thought the video merely reflected what he would be saying in his testimony. If you're not physically present when talented videotape editors shade colors, squeeze images, and manipulate video images on the expensive machines in post-production houses, you assume that the information presented is accurate. And in most if not all cases, trained legal experts don't stand alongside the editors to make sure the integrity of the images is maintained. This is problematic. The use of video in the courtroom has grown common. When the images are straightforward and clear and when the defense is given the opportunity to produce its own video or critique the one in evidence, video can be very effective. But courts must know its limitations and be wary. Or, as in the Krone case, someone could be sent to death based on the same visual tricks we use to advertise hemorrhoid medication. It is also possible that Dr. Rawson's tape was erroneous because of an early forensics mistake.

Dr. Rawson could see Plourd's questions coming and produced a new video for the second trial.

In the course of his trial preparation, Chris Plourd made another discovery. When Dr. Piakis got the case he took photographs of the bite marks so the experts could make overlays of the teeth and compare them one to one. They also made a mold of the bite mark to get a three-dimensional representation. First they made a rubber mold with the impression material and then they fashioned a stone model, the kind you see in dentists's offices, that would be representative of what the bite mark area looked like. Dr. Rawson made his own models after Piakis.

According to Chris Plourd, "They actually cut the breast off, excised it and preserved it in Formalin. Then they used that and the teeth kind of matched up to that to some extent."

But there was more. "What I learned, and this is something that has never happened before, was when Ray was arrested he was arrested very quickly. They actually took his teeth cast and pressed it into the dead body to show how they matched. They actually made indentations. This is what we've been able to prove."

A living body's tissue is resilient. It bounces back to its original shape after being compressed. But a dead body loses that elasticity and pressing the mold onto the skin would leave its own set of marks. When used later in trial or in the video, placing the dentist's mold on top of the indentations would not be matching Ray's teeth with the bite marks on Kim's body; they would be matching their own indentations which had been applied by Dr. Piakis shortly after the crime.

We have no reason to think the second round of indentations were anything but an accident or a mistake at the scene performed by someone who didn't have adequate experience. But the error wasn't caught by the system. Forensic science had intruded upon the facts and created its own evidence on the corpse and in so doing convicted Ray Krone.

What safety net should have picked the error up? Again, the system depends upon the defense lawyer to question, study, investigate, and challenge the evidence against his client. He can call his own experts and commission his own tests. But for the adversarial system to work, he must be qualified and supported by resources similar to those available to the prosecution. If defense attorney Jones had called Dr. Sperber to the stand, perhaps he would have inspired further investigation or closer examination of the video or at least created a doubt in the jury's mind. He did not.

Chris Plourd's re-examination of the evidence against Ray Krone rolled on, and he found more mistakes. Many of the problems fell upon the Phoenix Crime Lab, circa 1991.

"There was a new guy," Plourd said, "that did all the forensic serological work and he did a terrible job. He made a number of mistakes, manipulated some data. And when I got all his bench notes . . . there [were] all kinds of exculpatory information in the biological evidence."

First, more than fifty fingerprints had been taken

from the bathroom and kitchen but none of them matched Ray Krone. One palm print on the sink faucet was very clear, another on the towel rack and condom machine. But they were not Ray's. There was no fingerprint that placed Ray at the scene.

Second, footprints. Kim Ancona had just cleaned up, wiping the bar down along with the bathroom sink and faucets. She was supposed to close at 1:00 A.M., but before that, around 9 P.M., a man came in to mop the floors. He told police that he cleaned the bucket and then filled it with fresh water and new detergent so Kim could do a final mop behind the bar and in the bathroom. He said his job was to get it prepped for her.

Chris Plourd noted that when police came in they found a dirty mop and bucket. Kim apparently had already mopped and cleaned the bar when the killer appeared. There were only two sets of shoe prints in the bar, which were revealed by a special light, the same way blacklight brings out bloodstains dampened by the chemical luminol. Investigators said they were some of the best impressions they had ever seen. Rubber soles on newly mopped tile left clear, sharp images.

Kim Ancona wore a specific kind of shoe. They found her shoe impression and a second impression, made by a pair of Converse shoes. The word *Cons* came through in the print so they knew the exact shoe immediately. It measured between 9 and a half and 10 and a half. It was an easy jump to search Ray's closet to see what kind of shoe he wore. He has similar shoes, Mac-Gregors, but no Converse. And he wears a size 11 and a half.

Instead of excluding what they had found at Ray's apartment, the police argued he must have thrown away his shoes, the murder shoes. The report showed that Ray's shoe size was consistent with those found at the crime scene.

Third, hairs. The criminalist who did all the work testified in the first trial that Ray's hairs were consistent with the pubic hairs found on Kim Ancona's stomach. He was completely wrong.

Plourd reports: "I found before trial that the criminalist had never looked at the evidence hairs at all. He never checked 'em out. He checked out the reference samples of the victim and Ray Krone." Police had taken samples of Kim's hair from her corpse and samples of Ray Krone's head and pubic hairs. Those are the reference samples Plourd is referring to. They are not the actual evidence hairs that were found on Kim's body.

In a deposition the criminalist told Plourd, "Well, what I did was I looked at the reference samples for Miss Ancona and I looked at the reference sample of Mr. Krone and they were similar. They were both Caucasian so I concluded that neither one could be excluded, including Mr. Krone."

"But," Plourd continued, "he actually never looked at the evidence hairs, which is just total bogus fraud. That was his excuse."

What if the hairs found on Kim's stomach were not Caucasian but Hispanic or Negroid? Not only would they have excluded Ray Krone, they would have pointed investigators toward a new suspect who just might have been the real killer.

The prosecution knew they had a problem, so for the second trial they sent the evidence hair and the reference hair to the FBI lab in Virginia.

"Boom, a month later an opinion comes back," Plourd says. "Both Ancona and Krone are excluded as donors of the hair. They were able to classify the hairs as being from either an American Indian or a Hispanic individual. You know, different racial groups. They call it a Mongoloid feature. . . . so the FBI excluded the hairs."

Plourd was rolling, gathering evidence of his own by countering the first trial testimony and commissioning new tests. The hairs would not convict or acquit Ray Krone, but the prosecution would have to explain how hairs from a third individual were found on Kim Ancona's naked body after she had been stabbed to death.

Not only was Plourd building a new defense case, he was piecing together a picture of incompetence and outright fraud that combined to put a man on death row. What had driven it? Did the emotion that filled the courtroom for the first trial spur the prosecution team to do more than its best, pushing forward to ensure a victory by any means necessary? Prosecutors are driven by the desire to rid the streets of a killer and make a community safe again. It's a powerful motivation. Plus, every prosecutor feels the thrill of being placed in the hero's seat. Could any prosecutor stand up to those waiting for him to make the world better by convicting the accused? It would be very hard. Perhaps the prosecution in the Ray Krone case suffered from expectational bias—concentrating so hard on building a case against Krone that tunnel vision set in. It's human nature, and it would be acceptable if the defense also had a fair chance with equal resources. And if a life weren't at stake.

The fourth and final piece in Plourd's new defense case was DNA. The crime lab did test for DNA in the first trial. The lab sent swabs with DNA traces from the bite marks to the Analytical Genetic Testing Center in Denver, Colorado.

"They reported some erroneous results, in effect saying it was inconclusive," Plourd says. "Well, it really wasn't inconclusive. It actually was somewhat exculpatory. The defense lawyer [Jones] never understood that, so nobody called the DNA expert at [the first] trial, the prosecution or defense."

Plourd wanted a new test, but all the testing had used up the key evidence, the actual swab with the bite mark saliva. This was important, so Plourd tried again with a new technology called polymerase chain reaction (PCR). PCR had burst onto the criminal justice scene in 1992 as a major advance in DNA testing. It enables technicians to test very small amounts of genetic material. In effect, it amplifies or multiplies the sample so better testing can be done.

Using the small amount of saliva remaining from the bite mark swab, the lab came up with a 3,4 genotype, which was consistent with the victim.

Plourd was one of those lawyers who knew the DNA game cold. He was as much of a scientist as those who attended the forensic conventions. After all, he had to understand their testimony to use it in court. He had become knowledgeable enough to make his own judgments.

Those who work with DNA have a shorthand lexicon that makes communication easier. They talk in terms of types. Someone would be a 3,3 person, a 3,4.

"That was her type," Plourd said. "Ray was a DQA 3,3

but when you looked at the dot the four DQA typing was very, very pronounced. In other words, there was more DQA type four DNA than DQA type three DNA. So that was inconsistent with the mixture between a DQA 3,3 person and a DQA 3,4. There should have been more DQA 3,3 if it was Ray's DNA. So, my interpretation of the data was that this was a mixture. We knew the victim, the background from the victim's breast was a DQA 3,4 so you have to subtract that out. You're not looking for her DNA. You're looking for the saliva donor."

Plourd continued, "I said, 'We're looking for a DQA 4, 4 person.' You know, that's what the proper interpretation of this data is. It was not, in my view, properly reported by the forensic laboratory at the time of the trial because it was a relatively new test."

There was no sample remaining on the initial bite mark swab, so the lawyers started looking for other things to test. Their attention turned to Kim's pants and panties. The lab had found no blood on either item, and they also had not obtained a result from the black tank top Kim was wearing. Plourd wanted to test it again.

When the defense lawyer announced his intentions to test the tank top, the prosecution joined in. They sent it to their lab in Denver.

"I knew that lab person," Chris said. "And I said,

'They do good work. We should get good results.' And
they found some blood on the pants, on the inside of
the pants, on the pocket flap. And then they tested it
and it came back DQA genotype 4,4—exactly the person I was looking for."

It was someone *other* than Ray Krone (who was a
DQA 3,3) and other than Kim Ancona (who was a
DQA 3,4).

Everyone hears of the magical match in which DNA
identifies the killer. But perhaps the greatest benefit of
DNA is its use as an excluding device. Plourd hoped it
could exclude Ray Krone and therefore exonerate him
before his second trial.

The key thing was there were a couple of suspects who
appeared to be [of] American Indian ancestry. I
looked at some of the data that other crime labs were
starting to collect on various DNA types, and I found
that . . . 4, 4 DQA genotypes were very prominent in
the American Indian population. That isn't evidence
that you can bring to court, but it's something from an
investigative standpoint that certainly confirms the
premise that we are looking for an American Indian
suspect here. Plus there were witnesses who had seen
two or three American Indians, kicked out of the bar.
One was seen by a neighbor in the back of the bar in

the middle of the night. The DNA, the hairs, the witness account—it all added up to a suspect who was of American-Indian ancestry.

Meanwhile, the forensic evidence continued to build up.

"They did some additional testing known as a polymarker test and it came up with a genetic profile of somebody that was different than Ray Krone and different than the victim. So, it was not *her* blood and it was not *his* blood, and it's a few feet away. And I thought, 'No jury is gonna convict Ray Krone with this evidence,'" Chris Plourd concluded.

The new defense case was almost complete. It was far more impressive than the first trial. Against the state's two expert witnesses on the bite marks, the defense presented three. They were lined up to substantiate the DNA evidence and support Plourd's argument that Krone was nowhere near the crime scene when Kim was killed—that someone else must have killed her.

Unfortunately, they were up against the same brilliant prosecutor, Noel Levy. And as Ray Krone has pointed out, a trial is all about selling your case to the jury. As the flamboyant lawyer in the musical *Chicago* says, It's all about razzle-dazzle. And prosecutor Noel Levy was a very good salesman.

The new jury didn't buy the DNA argument that someone else must have committed Kim Ancona's murder. They also weren't convinced by Plourd's explanation of the bite mark evidence. Dr. Rawson's new video must have been equally impressive because the jurors had the same reaction as the first trial—that it was truth.

Chris Plourd remembered: "The way [Levy] sold it was—the bite mark fits, so there must be some innocuous explanation for the blood from this unknown person. And the jurors after the trial, that's what they said, 'Well, we checked the models and the teeth seemed to fit so we thought there must be some explanation for this blood that nobody knew.'"

Plourd said when he talked with jurors after the trial it was the matching of the mold to the indentations that swayed them. "They said, 'Look, the teeth do kind of fit in here.'" And so, yet again, the bite mark became the touchstone upon which every other piece of evidence would be measured.

Even Judge James E. McDougall, the presiding judge in this second trial, despite his own doubts, noted the following interpretation of the bite mark evidence and its impact on the jury: "When you actually compare the casts made of Mr. Krone's teeth with the mold made of the victim's breast, it is difficult not to conclude that

Mr. Krone's teeth made the marks on the breast. In fact that is what this Court believes the jury did in the end—simply compared the casts made from Mr. Krone's teeth to the mold made from the victim's breast and reached the conclusion that the 6,8,9 teeth matched, thereby establishing beyond a reasonable doubt that Ray Krone was the killer."*

According to Plourd, when he asked a juror about the blood on the pants that had a genetic profile that was different from Kim and Ray's type, "The juror said, 'Well, we figured there must be an explanation for it.' And another of the jurors said, 'Well, maybe she bought 'em at a rummage sale and they had blood on them.'

"I mean, how do you defeat that argument?" Plourd said. "How can you prove that didn't happen? I couldn't. I had several DNA experts testify and what have you ... "

His voice trailed off in frustration.

On April 12, 1996, after 600 exhibits and 38 witnesses the twelve-person jury found Ray Krone guilty of kidnapping and first-degree murder, for a second time.

---

*Special verdict, December 9, 1996, Superior Court of Arizona, Maricopa County, Hon. James E. McDougall. No–CR92–00212.

After the five-and-a-half-week trial, however, there was one person who saw through the circumstantial web thrown over the defendant: Maricopa County Superior Court Judge James McDougall, who had presided over the proceedings. The arguments that fell flat with the jury resonated with him. He was forced to follow the jury's findings, but he sentenced Ray to life in prison instead of death.

Judge McDougall told reporters he thought about calling for yet one more new trial after the second conviction, but he didn't know what new evidence could be introduced. "It's not easy to tell a jury you think they're wrong," he said.

What is particularly sobering is that the system was working as it was supposed to. The judge noted, "Although this Court finds lingering and residual doubt in this sentencing phase, this Court firmly believes the jury did its job well in conscientiously considering all the evidence and reaching a unanimous verdict in this case. The Court feels strongly that there *was* sufficient evidence upon which the jury could make a decision of guilt beyond a reasonable doubt in this case and their verdict will not be overturned by this court."

And yet we now know Ray Krone was innocent. Where did the system go wrong?

Ray's cousin Jim Rix and the defense attorneys continued to fight for Ray's release. It was harder because they had lost a second case, one which they should have won. Their hopes were crushed. It would take them six years to get another break.

It all hinged on the black tank top. In 1992, before the first trial, DNA testing was not fully developed. The tank top was also a difficult piece to test. As a bartender, Kim conversed with a lot of people—that's her job—and they sprayed saliva as they talked to her, which created a mixture of samples. It was hard to pinpoint anything from such faint tracings.

In 1999, Krone hired a third attorney, Alan Simpson, to help Plourd. Simpson filed papers for new DNA testing, centering around the left breast area of the tank top, the location of the bite attack. Surprising to all, the results came back with a good clean profile that didn't match Ray and didn't match the victim. It was an auspicious beginning.

The sample also had enough genetic markers to allow them to feed it into CODIS, the National Criminal Offender Database, a database that stores the DNA of sex offenders and other criminals. The database was not quite up and running smoothly in 1999, and so Plourd and Simpson had to sit back and wait. When it did become functional, CODIS recorded a hit between the tank top DNA and a sexual offender named Kenneth Phillips, who happened to live only 600 yards from the CBS lounge. Phillips was already in prison for a sex offense committed one month after Kim Ancona was murdered. His data had been entered into the system after his trial. "Once they got the hit on the tank top in 2002," said Chris Plourd, "they went to the blood on the pants and panties and they re-ran those samples. The same profile of Kenneth Phillips comes up. They had already matched Kenneth Phillips and then they said, 'Oh my God.'"

The authorities found Phillips in of all places, Florence, Arizona, the prison where Ray Krone had spent so many years on death row. They re-drew his blood to make sure there was no mistake in the database. He was type O. The killer was type O. The saliva donor was type O. (Ray was also type O, but so is 40 percent of the population.)

"Then they check his DQA type which is a different type and a different genetic marker from Ray Krone's. He's a DQA 4–4, exactly what [the killer] was thought to be by our side," Chris Plourd remembers.

Police went back and checked the fingerprints in the bathroom. They found a match to Kenneth Phillips. He had been there, washing the blood off himself as he stood above Kim Ancona's body splayed on the floor of the men's bathroom.

Six years almost to the day since his second conviction for kidnapping and murder, Ray Krone walked out of Arizona State Prison in Yuma into the warm Arizona sunshine. It was April 16, 2002, the end of a ten-year odyssey as an innocent man wrongfully convicted and placed behind bars, first on death row and then as a lifer.

Chris Plourd was there when Ray was released. "I drove over to walk Ray out of prison and there were five media trucks outside of Yuma. They all drove down from Phoenix."

Maricopa County Attorney Rick Romley acknowledged that Ray almost certainly did not sexually assault and kill Kim Ancona in 1991. And the new Phoenix police chief, Harold Hurtt, told the *Arizona Republic*, "He deserves an apology from us, that's for sure. A mistake was made here. What do you say to him? An injustice was done and we will try to do better. And we're sorry."

Ray Krone became the one hundredth inmate freed from death row since 1973 and the twelfth in which DNA testing played a substantial factor.

*

Is Ray Krone's case an aberration? Can we chalk his wrongful conviction up to a few mistakes within the criminal justice system that will never happen again? The chilling answer is no. DNA has opened a window into the workings of our criminal justice system, exposing its failings. The most relevant study of this problem comes from Columbia University School of Law. The findings are shocking. Professor James Liebman and his team of Professor Jeffrey Fagan and Dr. Valerie West found that mistakes like those made in Ray Krone's case occur in 68 percent of all death penalty cases in the United States. The Liebman report, issued June 12, 2000, states that "Courts found serious reversible error in nearly 7 of every 10 of the thousands of capital sentences that were fully reviewed during the period." That's 4,578 state capital cases between 1973 and 1995.

Professor Liebman's team further found, "There is a growing bipartisan consensus that flaws in America's death-penalty system have reached crisis proportions. It is collapsing under the weight of its own mistakes."*

*James Liebman, *A Broken System: Error Rates in Capital Cases, 1973–1995.*

CHAPTER 4

How Could This Have Happened?

Ray Krone's trial suffered from at least three of the errors most common to death penalty exoneration cases: prosecutors who suppress evidence that the defendant may be innocent; ineffective defense lawyers; and bad science used as evidence. Let's take a closer look at all three.

It is tempting to try to explain away all the mistakes in Ray Krone's trial by blaming Dr. Rawson's video, which so overwhelmed the juries in the two separate trials. Two defense lawyers, prosecutors, and two judges failed to catch its faulty production. Looking back, however, there were at least two opportunities to correct the mistake if only the rules provided by the criminal justice system had been followed.

First, the judge should have followed the discovery rules and not admitted the videotape at such a late date without giving the defense time to study it and prepare an answer. The appellate court said as much. We can only speculate, but the search for an expert to answer the tape might have led defense attorney Jones to the discovery that other forensic scientists disagreed with Rawson's opinion.

Second, something fishy was afoot in the prosecution's camp. Dr. Piakis learned early on that a highly respected forensic scientist and bite mark expert (his mentor Dr. Sperber) thought there was no match between Ray's bite mark and the one found on the breast of Kim Ancona. He knew at an early stage that it wasn't an open-and-shut case against Ray Krone. We can believe one of a couple of scenarios: 1) Dr. Piakis naively chose to ignore Dr. Sperber's opinion because it didn't help the prosecution's case, 2) Dr. Piakis "forgot" to tell the prosecutor, Noel Levy, or 3) Dr. Piakis told Levy, who chose to keep the information quiet, knowing it would severely weaken his case. Any of these choices was not only a mistake, but an ethical breach.

How does Mr. Levy explain what happened? He has chosen not to comment. Maricopa County is being sued by Ray Krone for wrongful incarceration and any admission of intentional suppression of evidence would clearly affect that lawsuit. However, in the interest of answering our question—How could this have happened?—let's explore some likely scenarios.

Clearly, the prosecution should have revealed its discovery of Dr. Sperber's opinion to the Court because it might have cleared the defendant. It's called exculpatory evidence and it should have been included in the list of every witness, every expert, every piece of evidence developed during the course of the Krone investigation. As we have discussed before, exculpatory evidence must be turned over to the other side during the process of discovery. Why? To avoid exactly what happened in the case of Ray Krone. Krone's case could have been resolved before it even went to trial—no million-dollar-plus cost to Maricopa County; no ten years in jail for Ray Krone. All they had to do was follow the rules. Detective Gregory would have been sent back to the CBS Lounge to keep searching for a different suspect and might have prevented the sexual assault by Kenneth Phillips a month after Kim Ancona was murdered. Instead, bad decisions set in motion a chain of errors from which there was no escape.

Let's put ourselves in the position of Noel Levy, the prosecutor. The pressure is intense. A young woman is murdered. The victim's family is in constant touch with his office, demanding vengeance. Reporters wait outside his office for a daily progress report. The community concern is broadcast on every newscast. The prosecutor's office takes on a boiler room atmosphere as the pressure rises to find the killer.

The public may still perceive the case as Kim Ancona's. But inside the prosecutor's office, it has become the case against Ray Krone. And the goal is to prove that Ray killed Kim. Some prosecutors put the victim's picture on their desk or on the wall to remind their team of why they are working so hard. Many prosecutors see themselves as champions of the victim and reflect it in their aggressive trial performance and investigative conduct. They want to win for the victim, the community, and themselves. Careers are not built on noble decisions to decline prosecution because of a lack of evidence.

Imagine, then, a moment when a prosecution team member—it could be Dr. Piakis—mentions that one of the most respected forensic bite mark experts in the country doesn't think Ray Krone's teeth match the bite on Kim's breast. Shock and dismay. They must then decide whether to start all over again or whether to continue forward. The case is 90 percent complete and the team is so convinced that Krone committed the murder, it's almost impossible to even consider an alternative.

Is Levy going to stop the investigation at the suggestion Krone didn't commit the crime and start looking
for another suspect? In our imaginary scenario, I think
the best guess is that he starts looking for another bite
mark expert and keeps quiet, hoping the defense counsel
doesn't find Dr. Sperber. His reasoning is simple: Finding an expert to support the defense is *their* problem.
Why should Levy do Jeffrey Jones's job for him? Besides,
Dr. Rawson may well be right, and Dr. Sperber wrong.

Investigative reporter Steve Weinberg, writing for the
Center for Public Integrity, reports that, since 1970,
there have been more than 2,000 cases of prosecutorial
misconduct in the United States that resulted in dis-
missed charges, reversed convictions, or reduced sentences. Weinberg writes, "Most of the nation's
approximately 30,000 local trial prosecutors strive to
balance their understandable desire to win—a desire
supported by the vast majority of the citizenry—with
their duty to ensure justice. There are some prosecutors,
however, who have exalted winning and ignored the
other half of the equation."*

Typical is the case of Gary Nelson, convicted of
sodomizing and killing a six-year-old girl. Nelson was

*Steven Weinberg, *Harmful Error: Investigating America's Local Prosecutors*
(Washington, D.C.: Center for Public Integrity, 2003).

convicted in 1980 and sentenced to death. In addition to having an incompetent defense lawyer, Nelson faced a prosecutor who kept evidence hidden that would have freed him.

The critical item of evidence was a hair found on the victim's body. The state's expert witness testified that the hair could have come from Nelson in addition to about 120 people in the entire Savannah area. Unknown to the defense, the hair sample had been examined not just by the state's expert but also by the FBI crime laboratory. The FBI concluded that the state's hair sample "is not suitable for significant comparison purposes." The FBI supervisor explained in a habeas corpus proceeding that limb hairs, in contrast to head hairs and pubic hairs, "lack sufficient individual microscopic characteristics to be used for significant comparison purposes and are so fine and small that they are unsuitable either to include or exclude a particular individual as the source of the hair."

The prosecution not only knew about the FBI report but did not disclose it to the defense. The prosecution argued that the FBI reports established not that the state's expert was incorrect but simply that the two experts disagreed. That not-so-little mistake sent an innocent man to death row.

The Georgia prosecutor should have known better.

In 1963, the U.S. Supreme Court established in *Brady v. Maryland* the "Brady violation," which stipulated that the failure of a prosecutor to turn over possibly exculpatory information to the defense would be considered reversible error. In 1991 the Georgia Supreme Court overturned Nelson's conviction and the state chose not to retry him due to lack of evidence and witnesses.

I often think about the moment in Ray Krone's case when the jury declared their verdict of guilty. As they celebrated their "win," someone in that courtroom besides Krone must have known it was the wrong decision. I wonder if they ever convinced themselves that Dr. Sperber's opinion really wouldn't have made much difference.

Fresh young prosecutors should read the Supreme Court's opinion in a similar fact situation in the 1935 case of *Burger V. United States,* which stated, "It is as much the duty of the prosecuting attorney to refrain from improper methods calculated to bring about a wrongful conviction as it is to use every legitimate means to bring about a just one ... a prosecutor's proper interest is not that he shall win a case, but that justice shall be done."

The Center for Public Integrity's article on prosecutorial misconduct makes a similar point: "The justice system is acknowledged by all its participants to be imperfect, and even when there is no misconduct, when there are no lapses—either intentional or unintentional—on the part of the police, the prosecutor, the judge, or the defense counsel, an innocent defendant can go to prison. At virtually any step in a trial, from the initial questioning of a suspect through the marshalling of forensic evidence and experts to closing arguments and appellate maneuvering, errors by the state—prosecutors and police—can convict the innocent."*

I would add that the risk of those errors is high. Add the likelihood of human error to the temptation of human behavior and you have a system that should not be trusted with rendering a judgment of life or death.

Jeffrey Jones must bear his share of the blame for Ray's problems. Granted, Jones was grossly underpaid and he was clearly sandbagged by Dr. Rawson's phony video; even an experienced trial lawyer like Chris Plourd didn't catch the manipulated video until it was too late. Still, Jones was an ineffective defense counsel. His worst mistake was to make such a bad choice for his bite mark expert. Perhaps if he had devoted more time to the case

*Weinberg, *Harmful Error.*

he would at least have discovered the American Academy of Forensic Sciences. These days any viewer of *Cold Case Files* would know where to go for expert testimony.

It's a shame. Jones genuinely wanted to help the accused. But he was clearly in over his head in the Ray Krone case, and his inexperience resulted in a death penalty conviction.

The Gary Nelson case shows us a more egregious level of defense attorney incompetence. After Nelson was apprehended and charged with killing the six-year-old Georgia girl in 1980 he was tried, found guilty of her murder, and sentenced to death—all in only two days.

Nelson's court-appointed lawyer, Howard McGlasson, was struggling with personal financial problems and a divorce, which certainly did not make Nelson's trial a priority. McGlasson was paid $15–20 an hour, and although this was his first capital case, his request for co-counsel was denied. During the death penalty phase, the defense attorney offered an eight-sentence argument on behalf of his client.

At trial Nelson insisted he had not been at the crime scene, claiming he had gone to visit a friend. In the short investigation by the defense attorney, his friend was not at home, but other people were there and McGlasson visited with them. When calling witnesses to the stand, McGlasson mistakenly called the friend who was not at home and had *not* seen Nelson that night, as opposed to the willing others who had. It ruined Nelson's opportunity for an alibi. In a two-day trial, there's not much room for error especially if the defense lawyer fails to ask for a recess so he can go find the other witnesses who would have provided an alibi.

In 1984, McGlasson was disbarred for mishandling a client's money.

The American Civil Liberties Union has written, "Ineffective counsel takes many forms including lack of preparation, failure to object to unreliable evidence, failure to present key evidence to the jury and conflict of interest."

In Illinois alone, Governor George Ryan noted that thirty-three of the more than 160 death row inmates were represented at trial by an attorney who was later disbarred or at some point suspended from practicing law. How does this happen?

One reason is that there is no special bar or set of qualifications for death row defense lawyers in most states. Any lawyer can try a capital case. Why is that? The medical profession recognizes that no individual doctor can be proficient in every medical problem or procedure. Orthopedists do not perform brain surgery.

Dermatologists don't deliver babies. Those physicians who choose to *specialize* are required to prove their competency before a peer board of review.

The legal profession offers specialty training in only a few areas. Northwestern University Law School's Professor Lawrence Marshall, founder of the Center on Wrongful Convictions, told us, "It is amazing to me that if I want to walk into tax court to dispute a hundred dollar tax issue, I can't do it, because we recognize that tax law is a specialty. If I want to argue about a patent, I can't do it because it's a specialty. But if I want to take a death penalty case all I need to show is that at some point or another, maybe 50 years ago, maybe yesterday, I passed the bar and I have a license to practice Law."*

The problem is especially acute in small jurisdictions, which don't have an abundance of lawyers from which to choose in cases of indigent defendants. Further, the community may never have had a capital case in its history. To expect family lawyers to become Perry Mason overnight is inviting trouble. It's a common problem.

Supreme Court Justice Ruth Bader Ginsburg has

*Kurtis Productions, conducting an interview for *The Death Penalty on Trial,* a special report for A&E Television.

said, "I have yet to see a death penalty case among the dozens coming to the Supreme Court on eve-of-execution stay applications in which the defendant was well represented . . . People who are well represented at trial do not get the death penalty."

Justice Sandra Day O'Connor echoed those feelings in a speech to Minnesota women lawyers: "Perhaps it's time to look at minimum standards for appointed counsel in death cases and adequate compensation for appointed counsel when they are used."

Another example of egregious representation is that of Federico Macias, who was convicted and given the death penalty in 1984 for bludgeoning a couple to death with a machete during a burglary gone awry in El Paso, Texas. At Macias's capital trial, he was represented by a court-appointed attorney who was paid only $11.84 per hour by the state and received only $500 for investigation and expert witness costs. Macias's lawyer failed to call available alibi witnesses, who would have placed Macias elsewhere during the murders, nor did he present evidence that a corroborating nine-year-old witness was not even at the Macias home on the day of the crime. The trial attorney neglected to cross-examine eyewitnesses or point out the lack of credibility of a jailhouse informant. He also made a false assumption about a key evidentiary point without doing the research that would have corrected his mistaken interpretation of the law. Macias's conviction was eventually reversed.

Is there a solution? Lawyers could argue this question forever, but most would agree that special skills are required to provide someone at risk of losing his life with a fair defense. The American Bar Association has issued guidelines for the appointment and performance of defense counsel in death penalty cases. These guidelines require the attorneys to have abilities, expertise, and skills in representing clients in capital cases. They recommend that two attorneys, an investigator, and a mitigation specialist be involved in every case. And they demand that full funding be provided to the defense and that statutory caps or flat fees be eliminated. But, according to the ABA, no state has adopted the standards.

It would not be fair to leave the impression that all states are ignoring the problem. Some have adopted remarkably progressive procedural changes. Indiana has adopted standards that provide a model for others to follow, even the ABA. And the Illinois Legislature, as a result of the recommendations made by Governor Ryan's blue-ribbon panel, adopted more than eighty reforms for death penalty cases in November, 2003. One of them requires special qualifications for death penalty lawyers.

How can we prevent such miscarriages of justice in the future? For one thing, judges need to be wary of fancy video presentations that can add too much extra "dazzle" in the razzle dazzle of a litigator's case. Someone expert in the nuances of television production should be available to make sure the images on the screen accurately represent reality. If we expect the defense to do it in rebuttal, then we must give them time and expertise to prepare.

The Ray Krone case is only one case, but I offer it as an illustration of the larger problem. Trying to assess guilt or innocence in any case is a very difficult job, fraught with errors that are going to occur whether lawyers are trained to perfection or not. The current criminal justice system may be the best way we have to make that determination, but it's not good enough to play God. We should not use it to send people to their deaths.

PART 2

Case 2: Thomas Kimbell

Yet the sad truth is that a cog in the machine often slips: memories fail; mistaken identifications are made; those who wield the power of life and death itself—the police officer, the witness, the prosecutor, the juror, and even the judge—become overzealous in [408 U.S. 238, 368] their concern that criminals be brought to justice. And at times there is a venal combination between the police and a witness.

FOREWORD, J. FRANK AND B. FRANK,
NOT GUILTY 11–12 (1957), QUOTED IN
JUSTICE WILLIAM O. DOUGLAS,
FURMAN V. GEORGIA, 1972

CHAPTER 5

The Crime

Thomas Kimbell's case did not turn on DNA revelations. It was an old-fashioned murder trial in which two separate juries looking at evidence that was 99 percent the same came to totally different conclusions. One jury tried to kill him. The other set him free. How could that happen? I decided to take a closer look at the evidence.

I lifted some 3 x 5 inch photographs labeled "defendant's exhibit" from a box of transcripts and interview reports that Kimbell's defense attorney Thomas Leslie had sent me.

The crime had taken place in the Shenango River Valley, where modest suburban-style homes have insinuated themselves among farms and cultivated fields. It makes for a chaotic land-use plan with fields of corn inevitably giving way to more lucrative residential real estate.

The photographs showed no tracts or full housing developments, just single-family homes. There were several aerial views of a red-roofed mobile home on Ambrosia Road, set back about 100 feet from highway 422.

The date was June 15, 1994. Judging from the shadows, it was about four or five in the afternoon.

A dozen cars were pulled onto the shoulder of the road and a crowd of people was gathered at the front door of the trailer. Even at this height—the aerial shots were taken from a state police helicopter, at least a thousand feet—you could tell it was a crime scene.

I had a strange feeling flipping through the snapshots. The photographer had studied and documented every object. The images drew me into another time and place, as if I were following the photographer around the scene. I was there.

A wide shot of the front of the trailer—we're walking toward the front door. To the right is a small blue plastic swimming pool for the two kids who lived here, Jacqueline, seven, and Heather, four. To the rear is a swing set. It anchors one corner of the lot, which is marked off in fluorescent yellow crime scene tape.

A hard-driven Chevrolet and an old Cadillac are parked in front, totems of a lifestyle on the margins. They're rust-pitted, their hub caps are missing, and the seat upholstery on the driver's side is worn out. In the back seat and on the floorboards of the Chevy are children's toys, a small plastic pink slipper and a discarded fast food container with the toothy grin of a cartoon character I don't recognize. There's a bloody smudge of a hand print on the hood.

One step up onto a small wooden deck and we're at the front screen door, aluminum, with a red circle of residue left behind by a forensics officer dusting for fingerprints.

The trailer is small for a family of two adults and two children. Closets are jammed with colorful soft dresses. Toys spill out from under beds.

In the next picture we enter the kitchen. It's a scene of violence.

The white enamel coating on the stove is streaked with blood that drips down the oven door. Blood spatters on the refrigerator and table, a shower of crimson on the white appliances. An arm intrudes into view, an adult arm. I can feel the photographer's reticence to move further in. He's accounted for most of the rooms, except the bathroom around the corner.

His pictures show just the floor first, awash in blood

edge to edge. And finally, a full frame shot from outside the bathroom door of children's bodies. The bodies are stacked on top of each other. The limbs are tangled. They are hard to distinguish in the caked blood that covers them. There are three bodies: the two children of Bonnie and Thomas Dryfuse and Thomas's niece, five-year-old Stephanie Herko, who had spent the night. The three are dressed to go swimming. They are slashed front and back, flesh opened down to the spine and ribs. Their throats are cut so deeply their heads are barely connected to their torsos. Arterial pumping has emptied their blood against the toilet, the walls, the floor vent, and the sink.

Bonnie Dryfuse, the mother, whose body is in the kitchen, received twenty-eight stab wounds. Jacqueline was stabbed fourteen times, Heather sixteen, and Stephanie six times.

Forensics estimate it took only three minutes to murder them all. This was a killing frenzy. What madness could have caused such an orgy of horror? Surely it could not be the work of a human being in his right mind.

I feel a visceral queasiness in my stomach as I look at the pictures. This is the only time I will study them. I can't go back to them, as if pulling them from their small manila envelopes would release evil.

*

The husband and father, Thomas "Jake" Dryfuse, was the first to discover the slaughter when he entered the mobile home at around three that afternoon. When police responded to his 911 call less than ten minutes later, they found him in clean clothes. There was a spot of blood on Jake's hand that he explained by saying he had bent over to touch one of the children thinking she may have been alive.

The killer almost certainly would have been soaked through with blood. Still, police suspected a case of spontaneous domestic homicide and centered their investigation on Jake Dryfuse. Detectives puzzled over the questions: Did Jake clean up and get rid of his bloody clothing before calling police? Or was he telling the truth? A private investigator, Kenneth L. Clifton, observed, "There was no sign of forced entry, there was no sign of ransacking, there was no sign of a theft. Bonnie's wedding ring was on the floor and there appeared to be an 'over kill' of the victims."

Friends and even relatives suspected that Jake did it. He was known to drink heavily and smoke marijuana. Bonnie had threatened to leave him unless he quit. In fact, Clifton discovered that Bonnie had told her sister-in-law Mary Herko that she knew she should take the kids and go to her parents' home in Kittanning, Pennsylvania.

Jake had also told a friend, Judy Fruehstorfer, that
Bonnie did not sleep with him the night before the
killings, which suggested that a major argument could
have simmered into the next day. When Jake walked in
the door that afternoon was he ready for a fight?

The case against Jake Dryfuse was fueled by a phone
call that his sister mentioned in an interview with
police, an account she would later change. Mary
Herko's daughter Stephanie was visiting the Dryfuse
girls the day of the murders. Mary said that she had
been on the phone with Bonnie Dryfuse from 2:05 to
2:25, talking about taking the children swimming. Bonnie suddenly said, "Got to go, *someone* just pulled up in
the driveway." In another interview with police several
months later, Mary Herko changed her story, claiming
that Bonnie Dryfuse actually said, "Got to go, *Jake's* just
pulled in the driveway." Had Bonnie's conscience
returned, pushing her to tell the truth? Or was she mis-
remembering? It's hard to know. Of course, she was dis-
traught at the loss of her own daughter as well as her
sister-in-law and nieces. In fact, her difficulty in testifying at the trial would indicate she never fully recovered
from the tragedy. Because of her emotional instability,
the defense would have a problem trying to present her
testimony on the stand. Her statement would become

the pivot point in reconstructing the 45 minutes in which the killings took place.

Bonnie Dryfuse was 5'4" and scaled in at around 250 pounds. Her dark hair fell to her neck, which emphasized a full, round face. She appeared large enough to put up a good fight against any assailant. Friends said she was a wonderful, almost obsessive mother who denied her children nothing, but added that she could be a formidable woman when challenged. One could imagine her reacting like a threatened grizzly if her children were in danger.

Bonnie definitely put up a fight against her assailant. At first, investigators thought slashes in the ceiling above the kitchen table were caused by a knife, but after checking the legs of a kitchen chair they realized Bonnie may have swung the chair in defense. Her left hand was sliced across the fingers and palm as if she had held up her arm to try to stop someone from cutting her.

Bonnie's wedding ring was found on the floor beside the laundry room door, leading investigator Clifton to speculate that she had been trying to make a point with it. Perhaps she had been in the middle of an argument and taken it off, saying, "It's over, our marriage is dead!" Or maybe she had been begging for her life, saying, "If you want the marriage over, here's the ring back, just go!" The only person who would have been emotionally affected by such an act would have been her husband, Jake Dryfuse. One thing was clear: Bonnie would have had to deliberately remove the ring. She was too heavy, her hands too puffed up with the excessive weight, to allow it to casually drop off.

A friend, Robert Arrow, suspected that a domestic dispute spurred Jake to violence: "Jake gets home and the kids are bugging him about going swimming or something and Jake can't take it. He got mad and hit one of the girls. Then him and Bonnie got into it. And that's what started it." It was only a theory, but it came from Jake's best friend.

Another friend, Charles Trott, who had known Jake Dryfuse for twelve years, also thought Jake had committed the murders, stating, "Jake must have struck one of them [the children] and that enraged Bonnie and then Jake flew into an instant rage and killed all of them and then cleaned up afterward."

Jake's appearance contributed to the profile of a rebellious "outsider." His hair stretched down his large back and was often braided into a pony tail creating a rough "biker" look. His size was intimidating. Still, he had managed to provide Bonnie and the kids with creature comforts. Inside their bedroom, playthings and pretty clothes peeked out from every drawer, every corner.

Jake may have been a generous father, but the police theorists could also imagine Jake wild with murder in his eyes, slashing the air with a knife, then cutting Bonnie again and again. There are signs that great passion was driving the murderer. Far more force was used than was necessary to inflict death. As Bonnie lay on the floor in the bedroom the killer gutted her, delivering a final stab wound directly into her stomach and twisting the knife for effect. The killer wanted to make sure she died.

Investigators couldn't get past three questions about Jake Dryfuse that seemed insurmountable: (1) How could a husband and father have done this to his own children? (2) How could he have had enough time between 2:20 P.M. and 3:05 P.M. to dispose of his bloody clothes and wash the blood from his body? The clothes were never found. (3) Why were there no apparent scratches or cuts on Jake Dryfuse, which would have been there after such a fight?

The investigating troopers also faced the Jon-Benet Ramsey murder conundrum: Any fingerprints in the house could be explained—Jake Dryfuse lived there.

Compounding the neat case the police wanted to wrap together was some baffling forensic evidence. DNA tests found traces of Jacqueline's blood on Jake's hands. But Jake had told police he had only touched

Heather's arm, thinking she was alive. Did the inconsistency mean he was lying? On the other hand, how could he have touched any of the children or walked onto the bathroom floor without drenching himself in blood? Did his clean condition mean he had killed the four people then changed clothes, missing the small drop of blood on his hand which was tested for DNA? Or was there so much blood that it intermingled, making it possible that he got Jacqueline's blood on his hand even though he was touching Heather?

There were not enough answers to build a case for murder against Jake Dryfuse. The case went cool if not cold over the eighteen months after the crime was committed. When or why the focus shifted elsewhere is unclear to those outside the core investigators. It only revived when the chief investigator, Rich Matas, retired and was replaced by William Phillips. The case needed some new life, a few breaks, and higher authorities may have hoped that Phillips could take it in a different direction. To Phillips, it also represented a big leap up the ladder if it could be solved.

Two names were at the top of Phillips's list of suspects: Thomas "Jake" Dryfuse, the husband and father, and Thomas Kimbell, a knock-around drug user who was always in the sights of the police, mostly for petty misdemeanors. Kimbell was one of those members of the community who always seemed to be underfoot. If someone asked for the "usual suspects," he would come to mind.

Kimbell had grown up with Phillips. They attended the same schools, and, according to Kimbell, Phillips had bullied him throughout most of his life.

It's easy to see why. Kimbell almost invites bullying. He is small, 5'4" and 120 pounds. He had always been small, a fact his father apparently found irritating and used to constantly berate him about. A lot of people did. He was not someone people stay around long. Kimbell can't sit still. His hands and arms are in constant motion. His eyes dart over the room, looking for nothing in particular, just moving. The condition is Attention Deficit Hyperactivity Disorder (ADHD), a hyperactive state recognized mostly in children and often ignored in adults. The result is often isolation from friends, strangers, even family.

Thomas Kimbell was also diagnosed as having a borderline personality disorder, according to forensic pathologist Dr. Bennet Omalu. This meant that he would change his demeanor for the slightest unexpected reason. His sister Beverly describes Tom yelling at her one minute and then sweetly asking some innocuous question the next. Does that mean he was capable of exploding in violent rage against Bonnie Dryfuse? It was never shown that Kimbell even knew Bonnie.

Kimbell had a history of anger management and psychiatric problems that could have made him a poster boy for the local community health services. He'd been around the services so much that a lot of people knew him. Many thought of Tommy as just goofy, not as a dangerous threat.

When I sat across the table from Thomas Kimbell in attorney Thomas Leslie's office, he struck me as immature, like a teenager longing to go his own way, tired of sitting with the grown-ups. When Beverly began to touch on something he wanted to say, he would throw up his hands, his face contorting in a little brother's frustration, as if the interruption had happened before.

Beverly was Kimbell's primary care giver. He had been married and divorced. She drove him into town to find an apartment, explained his incomplete statements to people, and made sure he was eating properly. She cared for him with the devotion of a big sister. She must have found it frustrating most of the time, but her tears came easily when she spoke of what he'd been through.

Defense attorney Thomas Leslie describes his client as one of the throwaway people, who could be discarded without being missed. Kimbell is among the people for whom the so-called safety net was made. It becomes their home because it's the only place where they are really wanted, where they can be with other people like them who understand what it's like to be very, very different. To many people, they are the losers in life.

Eighteen months after the murders, facing a dearth of good leads and perhaps the realization there wasn't enough evidence to go after Jake Dryfuse, Chief Investigator William Phillips focused his team on building a case against Tom Kimbell. His efforts paid off. On December 23, 1996, two and a half years after the killings, District Attorney Matthew T. Mangino announced charges of four counts of murder against Thomas Kimbell, thirty-five, of Ellwood City, Pulaski Township, about eight miles north of New Castle, Pa. It would be another two years before Kimbell would go to trial.

For years, defense attorney Thomas Leslie had turned down other requests by the court to represent indigent clients; he couldn't keep a practice going on the $35 an hour offered by the Commonwealth. But he was advised by a friend who was a prosecutor that this might be the one to accept. The case was circumstantial, his friend argued, so Leslie had a good chance to win it.

And you're not really a lawyer until you've tried a homicide case. It was time to give it a try.

Leslie considered the case before him. Investigators had found none of Kimbell's fingerprints or DNA at the murder scene. They had no murder weapon. The prosecution would probably find witnesses who would say they saw Kimbell at the scene or had heard him confess. But prosecutors would have to show that Kimbell had the opportunity to kill Bonnie and the girls and they would have to suggest a motive. And then they would have to sell that theory to the jury.

Circumstantial cases can best be described with a computer-age term: *virtual*. I like the *Oxford American*'s definition of virtual as "not physically existing as such but made to appear so." Applied to the law, a virtual case would be a case that is not necessarily true, but that *appears* to be so, or a case that points *indirectly* toward someone's guilt but does not conclusively prove it. The Kimbell case would prove to be a classic circumstantial case.

Thomas Leslie accepted the case to defend Thomas Kimbell against four counts of murder.

In the spring Pennsylvania begins a remarkable transformation from colorless mounds of dull winter gray into vivid shades of green. Chartreuse buds gradually unfold into a deeper, richer green that sweeps over short hills of dense woods. In western Pennsylvania the hills roll in waves, plunging from a hilltop down toward a stream or river then immediately starting up again.

New Castle is nestled where two fast-flowing rivers come together, the Shenango and the Neshannock Creek. Violence runs deep in these hills. The French and Indian War General "Mad Anthony" Wayne defeated Chief Little Turtle at the Battle of Fallen Timbers in 1794 to open up the countryside to safe white settlement. In the late 18th century, these western reaches of one of the original thirteen colonies were donated to veterans of the Revolutionary War. Surveyors soon discovered that their earlier colleagues had made a surveying mistake and forgot to measure fifty acres near the junction of the rivers. That overlooked patch became the perfect site for a new center of trade and government—New Castle.

Today, New Castle is a capsule of another era: the industrial age. Giant rusty relics of Pennsylvania Steel stand empty along the river, huge hangar-like buildings long emptied of their pots of molten steel and changing shifts of dirty-faced men. A once thriving downtown core is being renovated in hopes it can again pulse with the heartbeat of the county seat. Handsome stone and brick buildings under renovation are trimmed with hanging baskets of flowers, a nice touch even though most of the stores have yet to fill with significant merchandise to compete with the mega mall of Wal-Mart, Lowes, and Sears out near the superhighway. New Castle is the story of every small town in America, once discarded, now struggling to survive against mall behemoths.

A beautiful gold cupola rises out of the trees atop a white columned courthouse built in 1850. The New Castle courthouse is situated on a hill as if to protect the pursuit of justice from the distractions of mundane commerce. This is where Thomas Kimbell would stand trial, in the courtroom of Judge Glenn McCracken, respected as a thorough judge who favors neither prosecution nor defense.

All parties were confident McCracken would preside over a fair trial. Before the trial began, the judge warned the gallery that he took his responsibility to ensure a just trial seriously. He told them, "I have the authority to hold people in contempt of court. We'll have a short hearing here, send them right over to the Lawrence County jail. I will do that if it is necessary."

Another indication of McCracken's no-nonsense style was that he barred television cameras from the hall outside the courtroom. Reporters could observe the proceedings, but they had to leave their equipment on the floor below to prevent even the slightest disruption of the trial.

Thomas Leslie knew the courtroom well. He'd appeared in Judge McCracken's domain for fourteen years on many different cases. He felt at home in the room with its light oak décor. Prosecution and defense tables just beyond the "bar" separating the public from the official participants faced a judge's bench raised high to observe everything that happened in the courtroom—and to let everyone know who was boss. The courtroom had the standard elements: a witness box beside the judge; the jury box where twelve citizens of the community would decide the fate of Thomas Kimbell; and the gallery for the public and press. The only difference from every other courtroom in America was its shape. A creative architect had avoided the traditional rectangle of a room by designing eight angles, which gave the room the more interesting shape of a stop sign.

All this was familiar to Thomas Leslie, but he was still nervous. It was his first homicide trial.

He would have been far more nervous if he had known that it was Anthony Krastek's eightieth homicide case. As senior deputy attorney general for the Commonwealth of Pennsylvania, Krastek had spent his career pursuing convictions for the Allegheny County district attorney in Pittsburgh. He had joined the attorney general's office in 1997, less than a year before he was assigned the Kimbell case. During those eighteen years with the DA Krastek was also the supervisor of sexual assault and child abuse cases. His terrain was big city and big crime. Anthony J. Krastek was a powerful, experienced trial lawyer who knew exactly how to discredit witnesses and how to sell his interpretation of a case in a dramatic, to-the-point, and often aggressive style. What trying eighty homicide cases gave Krastek was confidence, an important element when you're presenting a case to twelve strangers and also selling yourself to a jury. Like a horse, a jury can sense when someone is afraid. Confidence comes from knowing what to do and doing it well. And though Krastek had been given only three months to prepare for the Kimbell trial while still in his first year with the attorney general's office, he was brimming with confidence. He wanted to make sure his superiors knew they had chosen the right man for the most publicized murder trial in New Castle history.

Thomas Leslie couldn't have been more different. Soft-spoken and kindly, he had a tentative presence in the courtroom compared to Krastek's brashness. Where Krastek was Duquesne Law School, Leslie was Slippery

Rock University undergrad and Akron Law School. Krastek was Law Review; Leslie was night school. Krastek's career had been spent sending defendants to jail; Leslie was more of a hometown lawyer who counseled his clients to settle out of court where possible.

There were some similarities. Leslie had come to the law late in life after seventeen years teaching elementary school. Krastek had been a reporter before deciding that he was better suited for the law. A reporter lives life through others, an observer but not a full participant.

The match-up may have seemed unfair, especially where a life hung in the balance, but you never know how a jury will react to the big-city lawyer trying to stomp their hometown guy. Krastek was wary of creating the wrong impression. He knew any sign of an over-confident, big-city attitude could quickly make the jury rally to Leslie's rural, courtly style.

It would take Thomas Leslie a few weeks to gain *his* confidence. Defending someone for a contract violation or personal injury is one thing. Having someone's life in your hands is quite another. Leslie had no notion that the psychological and physical pressure would be so severe. Each night he reviewed the day's testimony and prepared for the next day's witnesses. Sometimes he also had to write motions to submit to the judge. That kept him working into the early hours of the morning.

Meanwhile, Anthony Krastek had a whole staff to prepare his motions. He also had two full-time investigators from the state troopers' office at his beck and call, supported by as many troopers from the New Castle barracks as they might need. Krastek's own staff of assistants would take care of the mundane tasks of researching case law and taking depositions, allowing him to concentrate on strategy and the most important question: How was he going to justify asking for the life of Thomas Kimbell?

Are those advantages greater than the presumption of innocence? Prosecutors would argue that their burden requires all the advantages they can get. But for the system to work properly, it needs a worthy adversary for the defense.

Many capital cases suffer from ineffective counsel, lawyers whose inaction or inexperience doesn't allow the defendant to get a fair trial. It is so common because there aren't many lawyers who train for the specialty of defending someone on trial for his life. The career path for a prosecutor is based on his guilty verdicts and it can lead to the governor's office. In a few cases, it has led to the White House.

A defense lawyer handles clients who don't have any money. That doesn't exactly attract the top 10 percent of law school graduates. How can we develop an adequate criminal defense bar when public defenders can't make enough money to stay in business long enough to gain the trial experience they need to face the top lawyers in a state? Everyone in the legal profession knows that defendants without money usually get what they can pay for—an inexperienced lawyer fresh out of law school or a court-appointed lawyer who doesn't have much of a practice. The poor performances are legendary. Defense lawyers have been caught using cocaine at the defense table, sleeping, failing to cross-examine witnesses, failing to call witnesses—in essence, failing to present a defense. Remember Governor Ryan's amazement at learning that half of Illinois' 300 capital cases were reversed for a new trial and that "thirty-three of the [150] Death Row inmates were represented at trial by an attorney who had later been disbarred or at some point suspended from practicing law"?

On the other hand, prosecutors *do* get the training on the job. Good trial lawyers can turn their skills into an art form, from the way they walk in front of the jury to knowing what *not* to ask a witness. But that comes with experience, which results from appearing in court before a judge and jury over and over again. Krastek's eighty homicide cases would qualify as a graduate degree.

If it seems like I'm setting up Thomas Leslie for a charge of ineffective counsel, that would be wrong.

Leslie is a good lawyer, and he learned quickly. My point is that defending a homicide case for the first time is akin to performing your first neurosurgery. You prepare all you can, but being there is still frightening. It's hard to focus on nuances in testimony and strategy of witnesses while at the same time thinking of something to say, let alone anticipating what's coming next.

Not surprisingly, Thomas Leslie failed to get traction from the first sound of the gavel in the opening session. Meanwhile, Anthony Krastek guided his witnesses skillfully through the prosecution's case. The jury responded with respect and reverence to the uniformed Pennsylvania state troopers whom Krastek called to the stand. Law enforcement officers have always carried enormous credibility in trials. This would change within just a few years, perhaps the result of trials like O. J. Simpson's or television shows like *Law and Order* and A&E's *Cold Case Files* that showed police could lie, too. But in the Kimbell case, the law enforcement officials made for powerful witnesses.

Things were not looking good for Kimbell. In the halls outside the courtroom, the court buffs were taking bets and sizing up their horses. Even at this early stage, before any evidence had been presented, it was Krastek v. Leslie and the odds heavily favored a guilty verdict.

CHAPTER 6

The Trial

Anthony Krastek had the advantage of knowing homicide trials inside out, but here he was stuck with a circumstantial case. He would have to construct a case on incomplete evidence, like building a bridge with holes in it. Still, he was confident that with a few strong witnesses and a nifty piece of evidence or two he could do the rest, which was to create a story that tied all the loose ends together. Winning was all about *pleading,* and Krastek knew how to spin a great tale.

Anthony Krastek's theory of what happened on that spring day in the Dryfuse home concentrated on the actions of Thomas Kimbell and what he told strangers later. Krastek painted a picture of "Tommy the junkie," high on crack and out of his already strange and shaky mind, watching the trailer from afar until it was safe to move closer. The three girls might have been playing outside, splashing in their blue plastic pool. Their laughter, Krastek surmised, floated the half mile across the field from the trailer to an old barn near the turn-off to Kimbell's mother's trailer park. That's where Kimbell was hiding.

Krastek wanted the jury to imagine a drugged-up Kimbell watching and listening, turning a large-blade knife over in his hand. Murdering the girls wasn't part of Kimbell's plan. All he wanted was to get high. He was desperately wondering where he could get more ammunition to blow his brains to feel the rush of a thousand orgasms in his veins.

When I visited the site where Kimbell was supposedly hiding, it was clear in an instant that he couldn't have heard or seen anything over the half-mile field. In addition to the distance, a row of large trees obscured the view, a fact that was pointed out by Leslie.

Next, Krastek needed a motive. Without a direct link between Kimbell and the Dryfuse family the only motive he could create was that of a Jekyll and Hyde personality. Sitting in front of the jury, Kimbell looked like a small, quiet, harmless creature, so Krastek had to

The Trial 143

convince the jury that he had been raging high on drugs and had turned into a monster. Only someone out of his mind, the prosecution argued, could have created the blood-splashed house of horror never seen, never imagined in rural Pennsylvania. How could one human being do that to another, to children? The answer had to be drugs. No one knows what drugs can do to release the most vile and horrific denizens within our souls. Krastek hoped the jury would believe that drugs had transformed Kimbell into a savage murderer. It was plausible.

But Krastek still couldn't sell his story without placing Tom Kimbell at the scene of the murders. For his most powerful ammunition, Krastek presented an array of witnesses who came forward with some impressive conversations involving Kimbell. Standing alone, they would appear to be street-corner talk, but from the witness stand they took on a seriousness that proved to be troublesome for the defendant.

One of the key prosecution witnesses was Gino Saponero, who said he had driven by the Dryfuse home at roughly the time of the murders. Although he was observing from 100 feet away while traveling along at 55 MPH, he said he could identify Thomas Kimbell standing at the driver's side of the parked Chevrolet in front of the Dryfuse trailer. Saponero testified that he then watched as Tommy walked around to the passenger side of the Chevy.

With the help of his investigator, Ken Clifton, Leslie pointed out that if Saponero had been traveling at 55 MPH he would have had only two seconds to see Kimbell, certainly not long enough to watch him walk around to the passenger's side and look in the window, which would have taken at least twelve to fifteen seconds.

The jury would have to believe Saponero or Kimbell. Who was mistaken? Who was lying?

Krastek's next witness was Donna Beck. The day after the killings, Donna had gone to visit a friend in the psychiatric unit of the St. Francis Hospital in New Castle. She found her friend in the smoking room with about twenty other people, including Thomas Kimbell. Donna testified that Kimbell told her he had been smoking crack the day before and in an effort to kick the habit he had checked himself into the psychiatric ward. The conversation in the smoking group turned to the murders. Ms. Beck remembers Kimbell saying, "That's what smoking a crack pipe will do to you ... it is not as easy to kill someone with a knife as you think."

He also told her that he had done something very terrible and that it was "really fucked up what he did and he had to get out of New Castle."

It's not hard to conclude that Kimbell had been talking about the killings. Murdering four people is in fact, "something very terrible." But what if Kimbell was referring to something else? The defense would later reveal that Kimbell had stolen his father's watch to pay for the crack cocaine and argued that he was referring to *that* act as the "something terrible" for which he had to get out of town. But Donna Beck was unaware of that detail. To her, it seemed that he was talking about the murders and she had her friend call the police.

The psych ward at St. Francis turned out to be the mother lode for the Pennsylvania State Police investigating the Dryfuse murders. Another witness, forty-five-year-old Jacqueline Bailey, was there from an overdose of Hydrocodone pills. She told investigators she had seen Kimbell stand up and say, "It's hard to do children, you know, stab children, because they wiggle too much and you hit bone."

She also said that Kimbell had said that "women should be beat at least once a day whether they need it or not, and if that didn't work, you should stab them."

Assuming Ms. Bailey's recollection was correct despite her foggy mental condition in a psychiatric ward, was Kimbell really speaking from experience? Had he said that "children are hard to kill because they wiggle too much" because he had just killed the Dryfuse children? Or was it just the loud-mouthed observation of a medicated junkie trying to make conversation with other mentally ill patients?

On cross-examination Leslie was able to elicit statements which indicated that Jacqueline Bailey had been in a fuzzy, drugged-up state. When Leslie asked her when she went into the hospital, she replied, "I don't remember what the date was. I had passed out from taking too many pills." She wasn't sure about the dates of the conversation with Kimbell, either.

Krastek also called a number of investigating officers to the stand. These were Pennsylvania state troopers who had responsibility for the case. Sixteen-year veteran patrol sergeant Theodore Swartzlander said the officers had first approached Kimbell about the theft of a bicycle at a fruit stand in the vicinity of the murders, not the homicides themselves. They found him at St. Francis Hospital.

In his initial interview Kimbell told Swartzlander that he had gotten home between 3:00 and 3:30 P.M. "He went into his parents' trailer and he advised he was listening to the scanner with his mother, and he told me the scanner was airing broadcasts relative to this incident," Swartzlander testified.

"I explained to him, Mr. Kimbell, that there was no specific broadcast by any officer specifically of what had occurred at that point in time in the day, and he just maintained that that's where he heard, on the scanner, of the killings."

On cross-examination Leslie got Swartzlander to admit that sometimes investigators would feed erroneous information to a suspect to see how they reacted. Leslie asked, "Had you reviewed those [scanner] tapes yourself?"

"Not personally," the trooper answered.

"So you didn't know what was on them at the time?"

"Not the exact words."

Swartzlander had been fishing in his interrogation with Tommy.

On direct examination, prosecutor Krastek asked Swartzlander if he had asked Kimbell how he lit his cigarettes.

Swartzlander testified that Kimbell replied that "he would turn the burner on the stove and light his cigarettes. He said that a lot of crack addicts lit their cigarettes this way, and after he said this, he giggled."

First officers at the Dryfuse house had found the burner on the stove turned on.

Krastek was slowly building his circumstantial case. He moved on to stronger accounts of what some called Kimbell's "confessions" made to another group of listeners, inmates in the Lawrence County Jail. These were very effective. One witness, Anthony Daniel De Fonde, was a drug buddy, apparently both a user and buyer of crack who was often with Tommy Kimbell during confrontations with drug dealers. He told the jury that Kimbell said, "I killed four people, what the fuck is one more? You know, he said it on more than one occasion." On another occasion while they were driving by the murder scene, De Fonde said, "I was sitting in the back seat, and it was dark, just got dark out, and he turned around and looked at me over his shoulder and he says 'right there's where I killed them people.'"

Thomas Leslie was armed for cross-examination, offering De Fonde a statement he had made to police when he was arrested on burglary charges five months earlier. Leslie asked, "Would you tell the jury what you told the police that statement was?"

"We drove past the trailer on 422," De Fonde read from the printed statement, "and he said, 'Right there is where it happened,' and I said, I said 'What (happened)?' He said, 'Where them people got killed.'"

Leslie continued, "Now, you would agree with me, would you not, that *that* statement is a whole lot different than what you said here today?"

"It is confused," answered De Fonde.

Both lawyers were making points. Krastek was presenting strong witnesses and Leslie was skillfully pointing out inconsistencies during cross-examination.

Another inmate, Ronald Folino, met Thomas Kimbell in the receiving unit of the Lawrence County Jail right after Kimbell was arrested for the murders. He testified: "We didn't say two words to either one of us, for like, the first part of the time I was in there, and I just asked him, I said, 'I wonder what they did with the guy that killed the little kids they brought in today, because I heard it on the radio.' And he just come right out and said, 'That's me.'"

Leslie handled the testimony deftly by pointing out that Kimbell was merely answering the question—he was in fact the man "they brought in today for killing the kids." That didn't mean that he had actually performed the murders.

Sonia Hasson, a sergeant at the Lawrence County Jail, said she observed a shouting match between Kimbell and a female inmate one day. The inmate, Betty Spencer, yelled at Kimbell, "Shut the fuck up, you're a baby killer." Hasson said the two yelled back and forth, and then Kimbell said, "Bitch, I'm accused of killing four, you're going to be my fifth."

Leslie emphasized that Kimbell had said, "I'm *accused* of killing four people."

Krastek was relying on a number of jailhouse informants. Such testimony is notoriously unreliable. The temptation is for witnesses to tell authorities what they want to hear in exchange for an expressed or perceived favor. For example, Kimbell's cellmate, Peter Michael Karenbauer, testified that Kimbell had admitted to killing Bonnie Dryfuse. Kimbell had told Karenbauer about how the kids had run and hidden, how he found them in the bathroom, and how they screamed when he killed them. On the stand, Karenbauer testified, "He described the wound on the one little girl, it went across and down, and he described the wounds, some of the wounds on Bonnie, her arms, when she tried to hit him with the chair."

This was the only time Leslie suspected the prosecution might have coached a witness by providing him with information that would sex up his testimony. Leslie thought the prosecution team had given Karenbauer the details about the chair to strengthen his story.

In cross-examination, Leslie got Karenbauer to admit the state troopers promised to speak "on his behalf" to the court if he was cooperative. Leslie later reflected, "I don't think what they did offer him amounted to anything, but it sounded like something to him."

The question for the jury was whether they should

believe the jailhouse snitches. It was hard to judge the context in which the "confessions" were made. Was this typical jailhouse banter? Were the informants making the confessions up to help themselves? On the other hand, put several of these statements together and they start to look like a formidable body of evidence against the defendant. And the jailbirds looked pretty respectable when they got to court. They seemed honest.

Studies indicate the opposite. Jailhouse witnesses are unreliable. In November, 2000, the *Chicago Tribune* examined the 285 death penalty convictions in Illinois in the twenty-two years since capital punishment was reinstated. Their reporters said, "Capital punishment in Illinois is a system so riddled with faulty evidence, unscrupulous trial tactics, and legal incompetence that justice has been forsaken." At least forty-six times, evidence against the defendant included a jailhouse snitch.

As a result of such investigations, more and more courts are recommending that jailhouse testimony not be admissible in capital cases. The questionable credibility of a jailhouse informant is too big a risk to be the basis for sending a man to his death.

One further piece of evidence may have strongly influenced the jury. The same graphic crime scene pictures which rattled me were kept from the jury for most of the trial. But when prosecutor Krastek wanted to settle the argument over the blood on Jake Dryfuse's hands, he asked the judge to admit into evidence the crime scene photos of the little girls' bodies. His objective was to show there was so much blood spurting over the bathroom it could easily have gotten on all the bodies, explaining the presence of Heather's blood on Jacqueline's body and then on Jake's hand.

It was clearly a difficult issue, which Judge McCracken acknowledged. In side bar conversations at the bench with all three men, including prosecutor Krastek and defense counsel Leslie, McCracken wrestled with the notion of letting the jury see what were clearly inflammatory pictures.

Krastek argued for admitting a few of them saying, "There is no way that anyone's description of the inside of that bathroom can adequately tell that jury that there is blood from all three of these victims everywhere over that bathroom, the walls, the toilet, each other . . . someone could *say* that, but it would only be a conclusion and it would pale in comparison to the evidentiary point that Mr. Leslie very artfully brought out. The only way that this jury can understand that that blood could be anybody's is to see the photographic evidence."

Leslie countered that the point could be made as effectively by experts describing the scene of the bloodbath. He went further: "That narrows this down to the point where the only reason you can get the same idea in, the same concept in, the only reason for then putting this photograph in is its prejudicial value, so that it can be waved around on closing argument to inflame the jury."

All three men knew that if those pictures reached the jury, the result would very likely be conviction. In Leslie's words, the photos would serve "the purpose of prejudicing the defendant by engendering in the minds of the jurors the thought that someone, i.e. the defendant, must pay for this ghastly crime."

Judge McCracken was visibly torn when he spoke to the lawyers.

This picture is clearly inflammatory. It is very inflammatory. We're talking about young girls here. The ages are on the record. The faces of two of them are showing. The wounds are showing. There is blood all over the place on the bodies, on the floor, on the commode, on the walls, on the toilet paper, clearly inflammatory . . . I think the picture, although inflammatory, is of much higher, better quality of evidence than someone's opinion. That's the reason it is inflammatory. Somebody describing this is bad enough, but a picture is even worse. . . . and to repeat a nonjudicial term, I think we do have to give some credence to the fact that a picture is worth a thousand words. So, what we have in the eyes of this Court is a dilemma. It is very inflammatory, but it is a very important issue.

He added, "I don't know that the Commonwealth has proven beyond a reasonable doubt that it is impossible that Tom Dryfuse didn't commit the killings. So, that's how important the issue is, and the verdict could very, very well turn on the fact that he said he touched Heather, but he has got Jackie's blood on his hands. Very important, and I think it would be unfair to handicap the Commonwealth by not letting this picture in for the jury to make a determination."

So there it was. The prosecutor got his pictures shown to the jury, ostensibly to prove a single point of evidence, but the result was to shock and appall the jury, turning them against Kimbell.

At the end of the prosecution's case, Krastek had scored two giant tactical coups. One involved the photographs, but even more important, he had won a ruling to prevent the defense counsel from cross-examining his own witness, Mary Herko, thus preventing the jury from hearing her statement that "Jake" was pulling in the driveway.

Krastek had presented his case well. He had shown

that Kimbell had a motive (drug deal gone bad) and the opportunity (witnesses saw him at the murder scene), and while he fell a bit short on the means (by not producing a murder weapon), he could sell that point to the jury. But he had to do more. He had to destroy the defense's story.

Leslie was presenting an alibi defense, meaning that he would show Kimbell was somewhere else at the time of the murders. Kimbell had said that he had gone into town to obtain crack cocaine and then returned to his mother's trailer in the Heritage Hills trailer park. He said he was at the trailer park at the time the murders occurred.

When she testified, Shirley Kimbell, Tommy's mother, supported her son's alibi, saying that he had been home the day of the murders from about 2 P.M. to about 5:15 P.M. The murders occurred sometime between 2 and 3 P.M.

Kimbell's sister, Ruth Brenner, testified she had called her mother, who handed the phone to Tommy, proving he was there.

A mother and sister speaking on behalf of their son and brother? What could be stronger? How do you attack that?

Krastek created the impression, as prosecutors do,

that these witnesses were biased in favor of their kin—that they were trying to save his life. Of course, they would lie for him!

Cross-examination is one of the fundamental tools of our legal system. A witness called by one side on direct examination is expected to testify favorably for that side's case. Cross-examination of that same witness by the opposing side affords an opportunity to challenge the testimony, to take away the *sales pitch* of a direct witness to ultimately reach a more accurate idea of the truth. Cross-examination may show that a witness is mistaken, lying, or forgetful, having given inconsistent statements to the police months, even years earlier. Which is the truthful recollection?

The law recognizes that the truth usually lies somewhere in between direct and cross. That's what the jury is left to decide using their collective experience to judge whether someone is lying or telling the truth.

To throw some doubt on Kimbell's alibi, Krastek called Richard Osborne, the manager of the trailer park, to testify that Tommy Kimbell was a public nuisance. He beat his mother up and was asked to leave the trailer park a couple days before the murders. That didn't mean Tommy hadn't come back to the trailers, just that he wasn't wanted there.

Krastek also wanted to show that Kimbell revealed in

several conversations later in the afternoon that he knew more about the murders than was public at the time. His investigators interviewed every possible witness who may have seen Kimbell in the trailer park that day.

They found a neighbor living near Tommy Kimbell's mother who said Kimbell had said the victims were children who were killed with a knife. Krastek maintained that information was not public at the time, just a few hours after the police arrived at the scene.

Leslie countered that Kimbell had heard those details on a police scanner at his mother's home. The Kimbells had the habit of listening to the excitement of the state police radio. They enjoyed the bulletins, barked through static, which reminded them of the old radio series *Gangbusters*.

Krastek retorted that none of the witnesses knew anything about a scanner. Kimbell hadn't mentioned it to them when he was talking about the murders.

One of Kimbell's mother's neighbors, Carol Porterfield, said she saw Kimbell at approximately 3:06 P.M. looking like he had just taken a shower and then again, at his mother's trailer around 4:30. They were all talking about the murders and what happened.

Krastek wanted the jury to think Tommy may have been washing the murder blood off. Leslie would show, however, that the water had been turned off in the trailer court and without water Kimbell could not have taken a shower. He may have looked disheveled with tousled hair, but he could not have been washing blood off. Could Carol Porterfield have been mistaken?

To Thomas Kimbell, it seemed that Krastek was twisting the testimony to the Commonwealth's advantage, making alibi eyewitnesses look like accomplices conspiring to help their friend's son. Kimbell's life was hanging on every witness, and here was Krastek, destroying the truth of their statements. But Krastek was acting precisely as a prosecutor always acts within the adversarial system. As the representative of the government, he vigorously presented the Commonwealth's position and its reasons for believing Thomas Kimbell committed the murders. He was doing his job.

After forty days of trial, the evidence in the Thomas Kimbell case was in. The tedious parade of witnesses was over and everyone was eager for the main event upon which the case would be determined, including the life of Thomas Kimbell—closing arguments.

There's a dramatic arc to a trial. Final arguments are the climax when the two lead actors—the prosecuting and defense attorneys—deliver monologues that sum up the witness testimony and physical evidence for the jury. This is each lawyer's opportunity to take the pieces of a puzzle and assemble it in front of the jury. It helps if the lawyer tells a reasonable story so the jury can have a structure of organization inside which they can fit the appropriate evidence.

In order to win, prosecutor Krastek had to *sell* his full and carefully constructed circumstantial case to the jury. To do so, he had to create a persuasive story, within acceptable limits. Lawyers aren't allowed to develop a novella in closing arguments, of course; the judge will make sure they use only the evidence that has been admitted in court. In circumstantial cases, the prosecutor weaves together a nonfiction story tethered to reality by the bits and pieces of evidence each lawyer has introduced in court. From those observations by witnesses and physical items brought to court as exhibits, the lawyer tells a plausible tale, re-creating within the courtroom an image of what he thinks happened inside the Dryfuse trailer during those three minutes of terror.

The process is based, with a few twists, on rules as old as our English-speaking history. It's called the *common law,* the accumulation over centuries of thousands upon thousands of similar fact situations that have been adjudicated by judges and juries. Those legal experiences become a glimpse into the past, a fascinating collection of how human beings have struggled to live together and how they have solved their problems peacefully. From these observations of human experience, there have arisen certain procedures and rules that have proven to be our most reliable tools or assurances that only the *best* evidence will be used by the jury to determine the truth. We call them *rules of evidence.*

The self-examination that will come in the wake of the recent death row exonerations must reconsider all these rules of evidence and whether they really *are* filtering out the bad to reach the truth. Eyewitnesses have been shown to be notoriously unreliable. Jailhouse informants, while sometimes shockingly impressive, simply lie. Prosecutors step over the line to win victories while some defense attorneys don't even make it to the line of adequate representation.

In the case of the Thomas Kimbell trial, the two lawyers would be using the bits and pieces of evidence they had presented as well as some pieces they had squirreled away just for the occasion of their concluding remarks. It would be the performance of a lifetime for both attorneys.

On stage first was the attorney for the defense, Thomas W. Leslie. He softened the jury up with a recitation of their citizen's duty—perhaps the highest calling they would ever receive—to decide whether a man should live or die.

"What you must remember," Leslie began, "is that the law does not allow us to convict a person because we are shocked or angry or frustrated. The law requires proof that the person did it and proof beyond a reasonable doubt. All the anger and frustration in the world is not worth the conviction of an innocent man. Before a person can be deprived of their life, liberty or property, the law requires that he be found guilty beyond a reasonable doubt. That is not some trivial phrase from an ancient document. That is the foundation of our entire legal system."

At first blush it would seem the Thomas Kimbell case abounded with doubt. There were no eyewitnesses, no confession to proper authorities, no DNA link between the murders and the defendant.

While Anthony Krastek's mission was to build a house out of circumstantial evidence, inviting the jury to fill in important details, Leslie's job was to *tear down* the house or make sure it was never built. So he set about the business of casting doubt upon the witnesses presented by the prosecution and reminding the jury of the frailties of a circumstantial case. Leslie put it this way, "If you look outside and the ground is wet, the responsible presumption is that it rained, but maybe the water main broke. See, whenever you talk about circumstantial evidence, you will always have to be looking for, is this the only inference I can make? Are there other possibilities?"

Leslie provided those other possibilities with his alibi defense. If the jury believed Kimbell's neighbors and relatives, including his mother and sister, who testified that Kimbell was in the trailer park at the time of the killings, they would also believe he couldn't have been the killer. The alibi seemed tight. It's hard for a jury to look at a mother who's been sitting with them for five weeks and send her son to death. To do so, the jury would have to call her a liar.

Leslie moved to a key prosecution point—that Kimbell knew details of the crime not yet made public. "The prosecution would like you to believe that Tommy Kimbell knew too much too soon and was aware of facts that only the perpetrator of the crime would know," Leslie told the jury. "The fact of the matter is there was all kinds of information out there by that time." Kimbell's mother had a police scanner, and Kimbell had talked with Robert Patrick, an emergency medical technician, in the trailer court within an hour and fifteen minutes of when the crime occurred.

Leslie also pointed out that the police did not record their interrogations of Kimbell, but simply took notes. This gave him an opportunity to challenge the police techniques, which may have turned up bad evidence, now a common criticism in death row exonerations.

In reading the transcript, it seems that Thomas Leslie was drifting toward a common defense mistake. In his closing remarks, Leslie did not have to *prove* anything. But he had to make sure the prosecutor didn't prove his case either. He had to prevent the prosecution from successfully stringing together a number of out-of-context statements, which would make any saint look like a serial killer. He knew the prosecution would weave a tapestry out of the "bits and pieces" of conversations, fleeting glances, and late-night confidences reported by various unreliable witnesses in mental wards and prison cells. And so Leslie set about challenging the evidence and trying to discredit the witnesses.

Leslie's presentation was academic and precise. He tried to deal with every witness and answer every point that might have resonated with the jury. He attacked the jailhouse witnesses, saying, "When you think about a convict testifying, think about what kind of deal they can get—consider that—you can consider that in considering their testimony. What was their motive? What did they have to gain? What did they have to lose . . . the better he can do for the Commonwealth, the better *he* can do, the better are his chances."

Leslie continued, "The prosecution in this case has taken idle comments, statements of inmates wanting to buy something from the Commonwealth—their own self-interest without regard for the life of another. Is that how you prove guilt beyond a reasonable doubt?"

Thomas Leslie knew every witness, every nuance of testimony that had consumed his life for the last few years. He wanted to get it all in his closing arguments, not miss a thing. He presented the case for Kimbell the way a history teacher lays out differing opinions of an historical event, leaving the conclusion to the students. Such a tactic runs the risk of violating a basic tenet of public speaking, which is to organize your thoughts so they flow into a coherent storyline, one that the jury can remember. If you don't, you can bet your opponent will.

"The important thing for you to think about," Leslie told the jury, "is that your view of what you saw and what you heard is what is important . . . if you remember something that was given as testimony that's different than what I tell you, it is your understanding, it is what *you* heard that counts."

Leslie's argument was refreshingly honest, but it may not have been as effective as simply telling the jury directly what to think and believe in a strong, passionate, confident way. The jury is under pressure. The jury wants hard facts to help them in the most important task of their lives. And so, a lawyer must be concise, clear, to the point, and laser focused. The challenge for a lawyer in the arena is to make a jury think the way he thinks.

Leslie was handicapped. He was not able to talk much about his client because he had decided not to put Kimbell on the stand until the sentencing phase. He was afraid that Kimbell's history of minor crimes, crack cocaine use, and almost daily contact with drug dealers and junkies would provide the prosecution with too much ammunition on cross-examination, too much fuel for the closing arguments.

It's hard to know whether or not the jury wanted to hear from the accused. Some jurors like to hear a denial from the defendant's own mouth. In the Kimbell trial, it probably made no difference. Leslie was left without his most effective evidence anyway. He couldn't mention the name of the man almost everyone thought was the real killer, Jake Dryfuse, in the context of the final conversation between Bonnie Dryfuse and Mary Herko. It was a strictly technical ruling by Judge McCracken, following the rule of evidence that a lawyer can't cross-examine his own witness, in other words, prompt her and try to put words into her mouth. Instead of being able to argue that Mary Herko may have been naming her killer when she told police in one of her interviews, "Got to go, *Jake's* just pulled in the driveway," Leslie was left with the more general comment Mary changed for police later: "Got to go, *someone's* just pulled in the driveway."

And so, instead of constructing an alternative version of the murder scene with Jake Dryfuse as the star, Leslie could only ask the jury a series of open-ended questions: "Who was in that car that pulled up at 2:20? What did they want? Why is there not one fiber, not one hair, not one bit of blood or a fingerprint, nothing, nothing found, not one bit of physical evidence that connects Tommy Kimbell with the crime? It is a puzzle. It is a puzzle that the state police have tried to put together and it would appear to make the pieces fit."

He said, "They have shaved some of the edges a little bit here, a little bit there, but folks, it doesn't fit. It doesn't fit."

Leslie's argument cut deeply into the prosecution's case. He raised very good questions that ate away at the gaps in the circumstantial case against Tommy Kimbell. Would he be able to create enough doubt to save Kimbell's life?

The lime oak courtroom sighed in relief at the end of Thomas Leslie's hour-and-a-half closing argument.

Judge McCracken called for a brief recess, after which the prosecution would present its closing.

Kimbell's family had been there for most of the trial. Tommy's ex-wife, Connie, sat behind him, her face clouded with emotion. The Kimbells' hopes were high after Leslie's closing arguments. Thomas Kimbell didn't think there was a chance in the world that he would be convicted of murder. But he hadn't heard Anthony Krastek yet.

Krastek started with a friendly, soft approach: "Every day I drive to this courthouse and I pass the different roads and sceneries. The forsythia have dropped their leaves and the magnolia is next. The azaleas now are in full bloom. Perhaps you're like me. When you see the earth turn at this time towards summer, you're a child again, eternal youth, and you think school's going to be done, and you think of all the things as a child you got to do."

Krastek quickly dropped the hammer: "I submit to you, ladies and gentlemen, that those are the things that Heather, Jackie and Stephanie will never do again, and that Bonnie Dryfuse will never again rest her arms on that door and see if her children and her niece are okay, and the reason that is so is because this man killed them."

Krastek was pointing at Kimbell. He had set his course, a strong, simple one: The demon is Thomas

Kimbell. It was a classic technique for an opener: Spell out exactly what your intentions are in a simple structure that's organized and easy to follow.

Next, Krastek attacked Thomas Leslie. Leslie had tried to discredit the prosecution's witnesses, including the state troopers, in order to create reasonable doubt. And so Krastek attacked Leslie in order to buttress his witnesses:

> This isn't a game. Mr. Leslie is not simply saying that there's been some edges shaved. Before you accept that, understand exactly what that means. It means in a case, in this case, having seen those babies in that bathroom, having seen Bonnie Dryfuse on that kitchen floor the police are going to frame somebody? And then they're going to encourage perjury?
>
> Do you understand what he is saying, ladies and gentlemen? Not just that Trooper Matas, Trooper Phillips, Trooper Swartzlander, not just that these individuals—they're not some master cut-out uniform; they are human. . . . Mr. Leslie has done no less than accuse these people who you had a chance to see not as some cardboard cut-out, but in real life, has accused them of trying to kill somebody. He has accused them of being murderers, ladies and gentlemen. Can you believe that for a second?

We can see the advantage of the prosecutor. So far, Krastek hasn't mentioned any evidence. He's been swinging free, trying to distract the jury from the main crime by depicting his own witnesses as the victims. This is all an attempt to gain the sympathy of the jury.

Then, Krastek did exactly what Leslie feared—he reminded the jury of the gory pictures in lurid detail. "But again, the reason we introduced this picture was not to inflame you," said Krastek, "but to show you how these three babies were lying in each other's blood. That's a physical fact of this case. There's no way that you or I . . . could tell whose blood you would get on you when you touch all these spatters in here. There's pieces of hair lying here. There's a toilet bowl full of blood."

Prosecutor Krastek used the evidence available like a skilled carpenter. He was building his house. First, he demolished Leslie's structure and then began constructing his own. All he needs are a few pieces of evidence and he could construct a palace.

Krastek:

Now, the defense has said, "But it couldn't be Thomas Kimbell. It has to be wrong, because Thomas Kimbell was home." And Mr. Leslie said defensively, "Who do we spend our time with?" Well, I have no doubt Mr.

Leslie spends his time with his family, as do I, as do you.

Thomas Kimbell on June 15, 1994, is a crack head. He is trying to score crack. He has that urge. They have tried to suggest some idyllic afternoon of sandwiches and phone calls and lying on the floor.

Thomas Kimbell went that morning, blew off his meeting, and scored two rocks of crack, did it. He is coming down from that crack, and at the time, he goes by the trailer. He is coming down. He needs more crack, and as he goes by that trailer. Maybe in his mind he is trying to get a drug deal, as they have suggested—not that they have any obligation to prove anything, but they took the opportunity in their case to present evidence of why that must be so, why it must be so that Thomas Kimbell was not looking in the car outside the trailer, as Gino Saponero says, but instead, having some sandwiches with his mom.

The sarcasm oozed from those lines because Krastek was setting up the next argument, that all the defense witnesses were lying because they are related to Kimbell.

"I suggest this is the second oldest trick in the book, ladies and gentlemen. They get a sister—his sister—and his mom, and they go find their own records, their own records of where they were and then have them suggest,

well, at a time when I can prove where I was, I also saw
my brother, or I talked to my son. We presented to you
phone records of the calls that came from 100 Ambrosia
Road. Where were their records?"

Next, Krastek addressed Jacqueline Bailey's statement that she had heard Thomas Kimbell saying that it
was "hard to stab little kids because they wiggle so
much and you wind up hitting bone." "That is something a killer knows," said Krastek.

It is a description of his gut, his mind as he is slashing
those bodies.

No one knows this, ladies and gentlemen. You
know it now. The forensic pathologists know it and
they told you about it. This wasn't on any scanner. He
did not only fracture her skull—this being Heather
Dryfuse—and fracture the skull of her sister, but he
cut her with such force, used such force that he sliced
her across the back and cut through the bone. Mr.
Leslie has not suggested where that fact came from. It
came from the recollection, the tortured recollection
of the killer. It was the killer of those babies, ladies and
gentlemen, who told Jacqueline Bailey in that smoking
room it is hard to kill little kids because they wiggle so
much and you keep hitting bone. The killer kept hitting bone, and I have no doubts, and I doubt that you

do, about the screams and wiggling and every possible motion those little girls have made in that four-by-four bathroom.

Krastek was good. He told little stories with stark details that were easy to remember. He tied the evidence right back to his theory that Kimbell was the killer and showed how each witness fit into a whole story. Over five weeks, it's hard for a juror to listen to details from one witness, then switch to another witness and another subject and somehow fit them all into a general pattern. That's what closing arguments are all about. It's the wrap-up, the final story into which all those little details that seemed to mean nothing fit just perfectly.

And Krastek argued with strength and emotion.

A jury has to concentrate on the prosecutor's story, weigh it against the defense story they heard just a few hours ago, remember their assessments of each witness, their believability, and come to a conclusion. That's why closing arguments mean everything, why a sharp, talented speaker can shape the evidence any way he wants to go, and prevail.

Krastek was wrapping up:

We have his presence at the scene [drive-by witness who claims he saw Kimbell by the Chevy]. We have not a motive, but an explanation for such a horrible, otherwise inexplicable act [drug deal gone bad]. We have his statements, his statements of consciousness of guilt [Donna Beck], one story [after] another, and his statements where he actually admits this crime to people who have not gotten a single thing [jailhouse informants]. You have the defendant's confession all those times before you that he killed those babies and Bonnie Dryfuse.

On behalf of the Commonwealth and Bonnie Dryfuse and Heather Dryfuse, Jacqueline Dryfuse, and Stephanie Herko, I ask you to find the defendant guilty of first degree murder, four counts.

You could almost feel the energy dip in the room when Krastek sat down. Forceful and aggressive, he drove his arguments home.

The final arguments had taken up the daylight hours, and, as the glow of sunset outside the windows in the hallway passed into darkness, the regular employees of county offices were replaced by those interested in the Kimbell trial. Word spread that the jury was out. Some bet on the outcome: Ten dollars says he walks; I'll raise you twenty that he's on death row by morning.

Three hours and forty minutes later the jury returned with their verdict: four counts of murder in the first degree. It was over. The jury had believed the prosecution's story that Thomas H. Kimbell, Jr. was the killer.

Kimbell showed little emotion when the verdicts were read and the jury polled. He was stunned. He never thought he would hear guilty verdicts read with his name on them. He was handcuffed next to his counsel.

Kimbell's wife, Connie, started crying. "I love you," she said to Tommy. "I know you're innocent."

"I love you," Kimbell reportedly mouthed back.

Emotions boiled over. Connie Kimbell told the jury it let the real killer get away. She spit at Anthony Krastek and had to be pulled from the courtroom by the rest of the family.

Thomas Leslie experienced the same gut-wrenching shock as his client. "This was late in the evening when they came back," he said. "They do the guilty phase and then they do the penalty phase and they were out quite a while and they came back in with the death penalty and the judge sentenced him right then and there. And it was just terrifying. I have never ever felt that way and it wore on me for days. And then I had to have post-trial motions filed within ten days and I didn't want to touch anything. It was psychological. It was a problem."

Leslie had wanted to try a homicide case and he had chosen Thomas Kimbell's as his first. He had felt there was a good chance he could win it, and in the process he had convinced himself Kimbell was innocent on all counts. He knew that only he stood between life and death for Tommy, and he had failed. Before this case, he was not necessarily against the death penalty, but it turned him inside out.

Leslie still can't reflect on the moment without the emotion showing. "I know when I decided that the death penalty was wrong—when I was standing there listening to my client getting sentenced to death. I knew this was not right," he said. "This is wrong because at least this time, it didn't work. That's the point when I absolutely decided: It's just plain wrong. That, well, is the most terrifying experience I have ever had."

The Kimbell trial could have gone either way. Nothing in the evidentiary record provided an irrefutable link between the crime and the accused. The case was entirely circumstantial, which means little more than that the outcome depended on the talents of the opposing lawyers to convince the jury of their version of the events, their story.

The Broadway musical *Chicago* makes this point dramatically, that show business can play a significant role in murder trials. When Roxie Hart admits she's scared of facing murder charges, her lawyer, Billy Flynn, tells her, "You've got nothing to worry about, kid. It's all about show business, and I'm a star."

The reality is that there *is* an element of razzle-dazzle involved in trials, which can tip the scales of justice. It can come at any point, but it's most critical when evidence is admitted because that evidence becomes grist for the all-important final arguments, the clay to be molded by the attorneys into a sculpture of guilt or innocence. A good pleader can make the smallest piece of evidence seem important and literally "sell" his interpretation to a jury.

Anthony Krastek fought to keep out Mary Herko's key testimony, and it handcuffed Thomas Leslie. Krastek did it even though Mary Herko may have been providing the key to the murder. Did Krastek fight to exclude Herko's testimony because it would strengthen his case, or because he genuinely believed she was mistaken? Krastek also fought to introduce the bloody photographs of the little girls. He used them effectively before the jury. Was that fair?

The hard reality that shadowed the Kimbell trial, any trial, is that there is no perfect mechanism for determining guilt. The verdict comes down to the collective judgment of twelve people, a judgment that can never be perfect. When a case is based strictly on circumstantial evidence, the verdict is basically a guess. That is why a prosecutor should not seek the death penalty in such a case. We cannot and should not kill someone based on a guess.

CHAPTER 7

The Appeal

On his way to death row, Tommy Kimbell was still in shock. "I thought I was dying. I thought I was gonna end up dead. It's just, I mean I couldn't believe that the system let me down like this."

For the next four years, Kimbell would languish in prison. "People really need to hear about death row because you're confined to your cell," he said. "You got thick glass, bullet-proof glass. You got a steel door."

He was allowed to shower only three times a week. He was told when to eat, sleep, walk. He might have fallen into suicidal despair were it not for a remarkable man named Michael Travaglia, a fellow death row inmate. "He told me to get involved in Bible studies. He's such a good person he knew they had convicted the wrong man as well as a lot of other people up there. So, soon as he seen me he wanted to talk to me and said, 'I'm gonna help you.'"

Travaglia helped Kimbell write up his case and send it out to various law firms who might help his trial attorney, Thomas Leslie, on appeal.

Attorney Paul Titus from Pittsburgh read one letter from Travaglia and decided immediately that Kimbell was innocent. He asked to be appointed to help Leslie prepare for appeals. Meanwhile, Leslie had shaken off the psychological disappointment of the first trial and prepared eight issues to submit on appeal. As in most states, there is an automatic review in Pennsylvania for every death penalty case. Death is regarded as such a severe sentence, the system wants to make sure there are no mistakes in the process.

Leslie's appellate work did not pass muster before Judge McCracken, hardly a surprise since McCracken had made the original decisions being challenged. But then, the highest court in Pennsylvania stepped in. Defense Attorney Thomas Leslie argued his eight issues before the Supreme Court of Pennsylvania on March 7, 2000.

When Leslie appeared before the high court for oral arguments, he had a feeling the court was leaning his way. The justices didn't ask him a single question, but grilled the lawyer representing the Commonwealth during her fifteen-minute presentation. (Krastek had handed over the appellate duties to another lawyer from the attorney general's office.)

An appellate court does not review *all* the aspects of a trial from the performance of the attorneys to the credibility of the witnesses. It's not like the National Transportation Safety Board, which searches every piece of the wreckage for a clue to the cause of the accident. Actually, it's rare that anyone looks back closely at a trial. Transcripts are costly and are not routinely printed. The appellate court is reluctant to second-guess the trial judge, who they feel was in a much better position to make decisions. And appellate courts don't have much time for review. They have cases lined up outside the door, pressuring to get started. There isn't time to investigate every aspect of a trial.

What appeals courts do is review possible errors, usually decisions by the trial judge that may have led to an unfair and wrong verdict. On paper, this may sound good, but the result is a non-review of what is really happening in America's courtrooms. An impassioned advocate might sum it up this way: Lawyers blindly accept procedures and rules of the system without question, making them seem sacred, as if they are handed down like the Ten Commandments. As a result, certain mistakes are made again and again. It is standard practice to sentence someone to death based on eyewitness testimony that has proven to be unreliable and jailhouse informants who are, for the most part, untrustworthy because they stand to gain if they tell the state what it wants to hear. Prosecutors are so driven to win that they select only the evidence to prove their case instead of focusing on justice. Inexperienced or incompetent defense counsel plague the courtrooms. Questionable scientific evidence is admitted. A cult of authority pervades some courtrooms, cloaking law enforcement officials, experts, and even the judge with unfair importance or credibility. And finally, circumstantial cases are allowed, which produce, at best, an approximation of the truth.

Thomas Leslie presented eight issues to the Pennsylvania Supreme Court, such as the inflammatory photographs that Judge McCracken admitted into evidence. The court addressed only one of the eight. It would reverse and remand the case for a new trial based on the testimony of Mary Herko. It declined to deal with the other issues.

Justice Stephen A. Zappala of the Supreme Court wrote:

> The Commonwealth did not call Mary Herko as a witness at trial. She was called as a witness by defense counsel, as the statement would place Tom Dryfuse at the scene of the homicides forty minutes before the time that he testified to arriving at home. On direct examination by defense counsel, Herko testified that on the afternoon of the murders, she had spoken by telephone with Bonnie Dryfuse and that just before hanging up, Mrs. Dryfuse had said, "I got to go, somebody just pulled up in the driveway." Defense counsel then sought to question her about her prior statement to the State Police [which named Jake as the man pulling up in the driveway]. The prosecutor objected on the ground that defense counsel was seeking to impeach his own witness. The objection was sustained and defense counsel was not permitted to question Herko about the prior statement.

In his opinion, Justice Zappala explained the origins of the direct examination rule, which prohibits counsel from cross-examining his own witness. His explanation revealed the archaic nature of the rule. He wrote:

It is a relic of the primitive time when parties were not supported by witnesses in the modern sense of the word, but by "oath-helpers" whose function was not to attest to facts but the purely partisan one of swearing for the party calling them . . . Since these oath-helpers were ordinarily chosen by the party from among his own relatives, friends or adherents and countered by similar oath-helpers representing the other side, it was thought appropriate to regard each party as vouching for the credibility of his own witnesses and bound by what they affirmed. Courts have long recognized, however, that a strict application of the ancient voucher rule under the conditions of modern jurisprudence can lead to injustice, and so they have articulated and developed a number of exceptions to the rule, usually without questioning whether the rule itself remains a valid one.*

That is the reason Thomas Leslie could not ask Mary Herko a question as simple as, "But didn't you tell police a different story? Didn't you mention Jake's name as the one who drove in the driveway?" An ancient rule of the Middle Ages almost sent Thomas Kimbell to his

---

* *Commonwealth of Pennsylvania v. Thomas H. Kimbell Jr.*, October 19, 2000, Supreme Court of Pennsylvania, Eastern District.

death. And yet the rule against impeaching your own witness is in common usage in most jurisdictions in the country, embedded as an inviolate principle in the search for justice.

The Supreme Court granted a new trial. It noted that the Kimbell trial occurred in April of 1998 and that only six months later the court adopted new rules of evidence that now allow any party, including the party calling the witness, to impeach the credibility of a witness. The court addressed the issue of surprise: "The evolution of surprise from a requirement to be satisfied before impeachment of one's own witness to a 'technicality' reflects the difficulty in carrying on a traditional rule whose efficacy had diminished. The overriding principles of truth and justice have effectively dispensed with the element of surprise."

The Supreme Court reversal was a cause for celebration. It was one of several elements that would shift the advantage to the defense. In addition, Thomas Leslie had found his sea legs. The first trial had been a rehearsal for what would be a much fairer and balanced adversarial match-up. This time, Leslie would have the evidence advantage. He knew what the prosecution witnesses were going to say so he was ready for cross-examination. And he knew what to expect from his opponent, Anthony Krastek.

There was also a new judge. Judge Glenn McCracken's retirement came before the second trial began. Dominick Motto would preside over Kimbell's second trial.

Leslie got a better jury the second time around. They were intelligent, thoughtful, and not overly impressed with the uniforms of the Pennsylvania state police. This jury seemed to understand that police can lie or be mistaken on the stand. Leslie said, "The second time through, there were more indications that the State had targeted Tommy and a number of their witnesses testified differently."

For example, the testimony of the jailhouse informant Peter Michael Karenbauer had riveted the courtroom in the first trial. He had told the jury that Kimbell confessed to him when they shared a jail cell in 1996. According to Karenbauer, Kimbell said he had found the kids in the bathroom: "He screamed as he killed the kids. He said Bonnie tried to hit him with a chair in the kitchen but it got caught on the ceiling."

In the second trial, Karenbauer was afraid he could perjure himself, which might hurt his own appeal. Leslie recalls, "As he's walking down the aisle on his way to the stand, he said, 'You can call me to the stand but I'm telling you right now, they made me say those things. They're not true. I'm not going to testify to that.'"

Then, when Krastek asked him a question, Karenbauer

shouted, "I'm not going to answer that, I'm going to plead the Fifth Amendment." That was the end of his testimony.

Another witness, a neighbor of Mrs. Kimbell, said the police report was wrong. Thomas Leslie quoted her as saying, "I told the [police] those aren't my words. That's not what I said; those are words they wrote down. I told them to change it." Leslie said the witness was told if she didn't testify to what was in the police report she might be charged with something. When the witness was called to testify, Leslie asked the judge for a sidebar and told him, "I think she may say something different [from her testimony in the first trial], which may be perjury. She needs a lawyer to advise her of her rights before she says anything different."

The judge advised the witness to seek counsel before she testified. According to Leslie, she came back the next day and said, "'I'm going to tell the truth. I don't care what happens.' And she did. The jury liked her."

There was one new witness who bolstered the defense case immeasurably, forensic pathologist Dr. Bennet Omalu, M.D. A Nigerian-born modern crime specialist, Dr. Omalu was the closest thing to Sherlock Holmes anyone in New Castle had ever seen.

Omalu brought a new dimension of knowledge about homicide to the trial. He had expert qualifications in forensic pathology, neuropathology, and public health. He dissected the case as no one had done before, all spoken beautifully in an elegant British/Nigerian accent.

Omalu reflected on the case from the Pittsburgh office he shares with the renowned forensic pathologist Dr. Cyril Wecht. From the moment Leslie brought the case to him, he suspected that the murderer was not Thomas Kimbell, but Bonnie Dryfuse's husband, Thomas Dryfuse: "This was a woman who had two daughters and a niece in the same house," Omalu said. "What crossed my mind, there is terminology of intimate partner homicide ... Another is intra-family homicide. In the U.S. over one in three of the women who die in this country are killed by a former boyfriend or lover, a current lover, a husband, or someone who has been intimate."

During the trial, when the prosecution challenged Omalu's theory about intimate partner homicide, Omalu provided 250 articles to establish the forensic epidemiological basis, but Judge Motto still rejected it as not having adequate scientific acceptance.

Dr. Omalu had more tricks up his sleeve. "Bonnie Dryfuse was married to Thomas. He discovered the body. I asked, 'Did the police take any pictures of him at the crime scene?' This case had been tried and nobody had answered some of these questions."

Indeed, the Pennsylvania State Police had taken 450 pictures in all. Omalu examined them carefully. At one point he told Thomas Leslie and Leslie's new co-counsel Paul Titus, "Show me the hands of the suspects and I'll show you the hands of the killer."

They showed him a photograph that had been taken of the hands of Bonnie's husband, Jake, shortly after the murders. Dr. Omalu noted, "There were nail abrasions on the back of his hands showing a struggle. Another picture of his palms showed palms with a condition [abrasions and bruises] and I pointed it out to Leslie and he couldn't believe it."

At the time, state police had accepted Dryfuse's explanation that he scratched himself while working as a mechanic for his father.

"Pictures of Jake showed he suffered palm bruises," Omalu said. "He had blood samples under his nails. He said he got stains working on his car. I said show me the mechanics who work on cars who come home like that."

The police officer who had taken the pictures testified that when he took pictures the cuts didn't look fresh. Dr. Omalu said, "We blew them up and I said, 'They look fresh, recent. This is blood.'"

Dr. Omalu had also asked for a hemophilia analysis of Thomas Kimbell because he remembered reading that Kimbell said he was a bleeder, a hemophiliac. "I was hoping the hemophilia profile came back positively," he said, "because there was no way a hemophiliac could do this without sustaining injury on his palms. If the hands belonged to the husband and not Kimbell, he [Jake] did it."

The blood analysis showed that Thomas Kimbell was a moderate hemophiliac A. "When the results came in I called Leslie and said, 'Things are beginning to work out for us.'"

Omalu's testimony about the hands seemed to have an impact on the jury. "I was watching the jury when I said it was about the hands of Thomas Kimbell ... whoever owns those hands [Jake's hands in the pictures], did do it.

"Those hands of Jake were a good instrument for us. If Thomas Kimbell was agitated, in an explosive mood, his hands would have looked like these hands [Jake's]."

Omalu applied his theory to the facts of the case. "I told the prosecution, 'You think he cleaned up his clothes? I wouldn't think in the time frame he could successfully clean up clothes and hide the weapons to take a shower with nothing left on him.' It was true reasonable doubt."

Dr. Omalu also explored Kimbell's mental state:

"Kimbell is ADHD, borderline personality disorder, with a history of anger management, a long psychiatric history, an explosive disorder . . . if he was hemophiliac under cocaine then his judgment would be impaired.

"I asked the prosecution, 'Is it physically possible for someone of Thomas Kimbell's size and weight [100 lbs and 5'5"] to stab the woman and children so many times requiring energy and come out without impaired judgment, without any blood to be seen within one to two hours of the crime? That's impossible.'"

Dr. Omalu reasoned that it didn't make sense to argue that Kimbell was high on crack and then exploded in a rage to massacre four people. The doctor brought his research to bear: "We provided articles about the cocaine-induced state. These people are agitated. They lose their sense of judgment for days. How could he have left the scene, walked home, and successfully disposed of the clothing? Thomas Kimbell's mother said she saw him looking very calm, taking a shower in the evening. Everyone said he looked calm. Two days later he was in hospital and doctors said there was no evidence of trauma."

What Dr. Omalu argued was significant: (1) There was no evidence of significant trauma on Thomas Kimbell, (2) There was abundant evidence on the hands of

Jake Dryfuse, (3) With such a degree of hemophilia there was no way Thomas Kimbell could have assaulted 250-pound Bonnie Dryfuse without sustaining injury.

Dr. Omalu had become convinced Jake Dryfuse was the murderer: "I'll bet my life Jake did it and his father knows. His mother is in absolute silence. His motive may be his marriage breaking up. He had a history of beating his last wife. So he had done it many times. He could have got into a desperate, hopeless mental state and murdered this woman. Killing for passion is often the motivation behind multiple stab wounds, inflicted without consequence when only one wound was necessary."

But there was one big question, which had loomed large in the first trial. How could Jake murder his children so brutally? Dr. Omalu had an answer: "Jake had greater emotional bonding to his two daughters. There was a niece. When you compare the pattern of trauma of his children with Stephanie, the niece, there were more stab wounds on his own children, more mutilation. He spent more time with his own children and less on Stephanie. She had one decisive gash of neck."

And Dr. Omalu's explanation? "Because of the greater emotional attachment the stab wounds are greater in number, up and down, part of my proposition for intimate family homicide."

Dr. Omalu's full testimony didn't have to be accepted

by the jury, just enough to create a reasonable doubt. But his answer to the question that had stumped everyone—How could Jake kill his own children?—was extremely interesting. And Thomas Leslie was able to use it. Leslie recalls: "What came out in the testimony was that it was more likely Jake did it than a complete stranger. A complete stranger, if they're going to kill someone, they kill them. If someone has some kind of emotional attachment, like that done here, it suggests Jake."

Thomas Leslie's biggest advantage came in the testimony of Mary Herko, the subject of the Supreme Court's reversal. When Herko fell apart on the stand, she was declared an unavailable witness and Leslie was allowed to play her videotape deposition, the same one that was used in the first trial but stopped just before she mentioned Jake's name. Leslie put the trooper who took the statement on the stand. "I asked about the statement and I played the statement so the jury actually heard it right from Mary Herko's mouth," Leslie said. "They heard the all-important comment, 'Got to go, Jake's just pulled in the driveway.'"

After a two-week trial, four years after he was sentenced to die for the four murders, the jury in the second trial acquitted Thomas Kimbell of all charges. They had deliberated for thirteen hours over two days.

It was May 3, 2002, and the reaction was strange. The Kimbell family was overjoyed, of course. But Mary Herko, already emotionally disturbed to the point of not being able to testify in person at the trial, lay down in the middle of a road near the courthouse and refused to move. Finally, a state trooper called an ambulance.

After the trial, Thomas Jake Dryfuse disappeared from New Castle and has not been seen since. No law enforcement authority has reopened the case.

When we ask again—how could it have happened?— the second trial stands as something of an answer. There was Mary Herko's testimony, which should have been allowed at the first trial. Or did Anthony Krastek's eyewitnesses, placing Thomas Kimbell at the murder scene, lose their credibility? And the jailhouse informants, did they suddenly turn from believable witnesses to liars looking for a payoff from the Commonwealth? Or was it Thomas Leslie's acquired confidence in his second homicide trial that enabled him to better handle the evidence against Kimbell and the aggressive style of Krastek? Or was it the different jury? It may have been Dr. Omalu's testimony that swayed the jury. He revealed an understanding of this type of homicide that was lacking in the first trial.

Most likely, it was the cumulative effect of all those things. But the reality is that we don't know for sure why the two Kimbell juries came to two different conclusions. And the legal profession is reticent to ask. It prefers to leave the answer in that mystical collective mind of twelve people and believe that somehow they know the truth.

If it weren't for DNA, we might continue to believe that magic happens behind those jury doors. But now we know there is no magical device to determine truth. U.S. Supreme Court Justice Harry Blackmun, in a dissenting opinion in 1994, *Callins v. James,* wrote: "The basic question—does the system accurately and consistently determine which defendants 'deserve to die'—cannot be answered in the affirmative. . . . The problem is that the inevitability of factual, legal and moral error gives us a system that we know must wrongly kill some defendants, a system that fails to deliver the fair, consistent, and reliable sentences required by the Constitution."

Justice Blackmun, after a lifetime of upholding the constitutionality of the death penalty, withdrew that support: "I feel morally and intellectually obligated simply to concede that the death penalty experiment has failed," he wrote.

Conclusion

We have journeyed through two exoneration cases in an effort to test Justice Marshall's assertion in the Introduction to this book that if we were better informed about the death penalty, we would consider it shocking, unjust, and unacceptable. What we have learned is that the criminal justice system is rife with the potential for error. As a result of DNA forcing the review of cases, the percentage of wrongful convictions is shockingly high.

There are other arguments against capital punishment that we did not focus on, but that should be noted.

It is not a deterrent to homicide.

Too much time has been wasted on this argument. I simply note what Justice Potter Stewart observed in *Furman v. Georgia:* Many statistical studies—comparing crime rates in jurisdictions with and without capital punishment and in jurisdictions before and after abolition of capital punishment—have indicated that there is little, if any, measurable deterrent effect. There are too many variables at play.

It is too expensive.

A North Carolina study ten years ago found the cost of a death penalty case was $2.16 million more per execution than per life sentence. And that included the cost of lifetime incarceration. In Texas, one death penalty case equals $2.3 million more than a non-death case. I visited one county in South Carolina that had to put off paving streets and repairing new sidewalks because of the costs of a death penalty trial, a trial in which the prosecutor did not even get a death sentence. Only 10 percent of death penalty cases actually end in execution. Today, governments are facing smaller and smaller budgets, causing legislators to ask, is the death penalty really worth it? Wouldn't that money be better spent on education, Medicaid, and highways?

It is unfairly applied among the states.

The death penalty applies to sixteen-year-olds in some states; in others, those found guilty have to be eighteen to qualify for the death penalty. Some states sentence criminals to life without parole, others do not. Some states require judges to inform juries that such an alternative exists, but more states (twenty-three out of twenty-nine that have life without parole) bar judges from giving such information to jurors. This is important because when given a choice between a sentence of death and a sentence of life without parole, most people will choose the latter.

On this argument, Justice Stewart wrote in *Furman*, "These death sentences are cruel and unusual in the same way that being struck by lightning is cruel and unusual . . . I simply conclude that the Eighth and Fourteenth Amendments cannot tolerate the infliction of a sentence of death under legal systems that permit this unique penalty to be so wantonly and so freakishly imposed." The *Furman* decision was in 1972, but the reasoning still applies today.

The death penalty is unfair to the poor and minorities.

A look at the bare statistics regarding executions is enough to make the point. A total of 3,859 persons have been executed since 1930, of whom 1,751 were white and 2,066 were black. Of the executions, 3,334 were for murder; 1,664 of the executed murderers were white and 1,630 were black; 455 persons, including 48 whites and 405 blacks, were executed for rape. Justice Thurgood Marshall has written, "It is usually the poor, the illiterate, the underprivileged, the member of the minority group—the man who, because he is without means, and is defended by a court-appointed attorney—who becomes society's sacrificial lamb . . . "*

The United States is out of touch with the global community.

The world has been watching America's dance with the death penalty for many years. The United States is one of the only developed countries that still uses the death penalty as a criminal punishment. All the European countries have abolished it. Of those countries that still execute people, China has the most executions every year, followed by Iraq, Iran, Saudi Arabia, and then America. The United States is also one of only six countries that sentence juveniles to death. Pakistan, Iran,

* *Furman v. Georgia*, 408 U.S. 238 (1972) concurring oinion.

Nigeria, Saudi Arabia, and Yemen complete the tight little fraternity.

The United Nations Commission on Human rights has urged the United States to change its position on capital punishment. It believes a nation that uses the death penalty must be a perfect one. And there are *no* perfect nations.

France refuses to extradite criminals to the United States if they face the death penalty here. Mexico is expected to soon follow suit. When will the issue spill over in the form of economic boycotts or sanctions imposed by the global market countries that feel they have grown beyond us morally?

Our system of jurisprudence has become institutionalized.

Judges and lawyers often act out of blind obedience to rules and procedures, doing things because they have always been done that way.

One of the most egregious examples involves the case of Joseph Amrine, who spent twenty-six years behind bars, eighteen of them on death row, for stabbing a fellow inmate to death in 1985. He was given an execution date four times, but it was always postponed.

Barbara Shelly reported for the *Kansas City Star* that an assistant to the Missouri Attorney General, Frank Jung, argued to the Missouri Supreme Court that they should concern themselves not with the mounting evidence of Amrine's innocence but only with whether his constitutional rights had been violated. In other words, the *process* was more important than innocence. On February 8, 2003, Shelly quoted the exchange before the Supreme Court.

"Is it not a cruel and unusual punishment to execute an innocent person?" a judge asked.

"If there is no underlying constitutional violation, there is not a right to relief," Jung said. "Even if DNA evidence conclusively found an inmate innocent, the court would need a constitutional violation to stop an execution. That's the standard, your honor."

A spokesman for the attorney general realized the position might appear ludicrous to the public and tried to explain that it's not the role of the appellate court to retry a case; that's the responsibility of the trial court and the jury. The appellate court, rather, considers trial errors and whether the defendant's right to a fair trial was violated. The assistant attorney general was more interested in doing things right than doing the right thing.

Let's pause a moment to consider. That twisted logic

can be heard over and over in legal debates that look so hard for resolution from inside a briar patch of interconnecting issues that the real goal—truth and justice—is not kept in consideration. The *institution* of justice has too often become more important than justice itself.

The Kimbell case was a prime example. As we saw, an archaic 500-year-old procedural rule was used to keep a critical piece of testimony from the jury—"Got to go, *Jake's* just pulled in the driveway." Fortunately, the Pennsylvania Supreme Court realized the error, though they wouldn't have reversed if the rule itself hadn't been removed from use in Pennsylvania six months after the first trial. How many other rules are out of date?

How do we correct the system? Perhaps we can learn from other organizations that have faced a similar problem. Let's think "outside the box."

After the Space Shuttle Columbia's accident that killed seven astronauts on February 1, 2003, a staff of 120 personnel conducted 200 formal interviews and reviewed more than 3,000 public inputs. The thirteen-member CAIB, Columbia Accident Investigation Board, produced an eleven-chapter, 250-page report. In the report, which has become a standard of excellence throughout government agencies, the CAIB wrote that NASA's *organizational culture* had as much to do with this accident as foam did: "Without addressing the culture, which perpetuated the problem," it wrote, "there could be no correction."

What did the board mean by blaming the culture? The CAIB wrote: "Organizational culture refers to the values, norms, beliefs and practices that govern how an institution functions. At the most basic level, organizational culture defines the assumptions that employees make as they carry out their work. It is a powerful force that can persist through reorganizations and the reassignment of key personnel."

Apply that same language to any system or bureaucracy that becomes mired in its own culture, including the legal profession.

The NASA investigation uncovered a troubling pattern in which Shuttle Program management made erroneous assumptions about the robustness of a system "based on prior success rather than on dependable engineering data and rigorous testing."

The criminal justice system has been operating on "prior success" for ages. At least we assumed the convictions were successful and the verdicts correct—until DNA made us realize our "prior success" was, in many cases, a sham.

One important question leapt out at me from the NASA report's pages: "Perhaps the most perplexing

question the Board faced during its seven month investigation into the Columbia accident was, how could
NASA have missed the signals the foam was sending?"

I ask, how can the *legal profession* miss the signals
that DNA is sending? How many death row inmates
have to be exonerated before we realize the risk of error
is too great to keep capital punishment on the statute
books? That question doesn't even begin to explore the
frightening question beyond death penalty convictions:
What about lesser cases? Do they also have a failure rate
of 68 percent?

While George Ryan was listening to the cheers across
Europe as he spread his mantra of "How could this have
happened?" his blue-ribbon commission not only delivered some answers but followed them through the Illinois Legislature. On January 20, 2004, the final
legislative package of capital punishment reforms was
signed into law by Governor Rod R. Blagojevich.
Although the reforms narrowed the conditions, we
must observe that once again, the criminal justice system dodged the bullet, allowing the death penalty to
remain on the books.

In the year after his dramatic decision to commute all
the sentences of Illinois' death row inmates, Governor

George Ryan became the darling of death penalty aboli-
tionists. In October, 2003, he found himself being
driven past the Roman Forum, around the Arch of
Titus, to the Coliseum itself, where the lights were
turned on just for him, an honor afforded only a few in
the style of a triumphant Roman emperor.

It was an accolade he would *not* receive in Illinois
despite the passage of his death penalty reforms. A team
of federal prosecutors was hot on Ryan's heels when he
left office in January, 2003. Many suspected that the day
after his opponent's inauguration he would be indicted
for a variety of violations committed years before during his tenure as Illinois Secretary of State. Instead,
prosecutors waited as long as they could, indicting Ryan
only a few days before the statute of limitations would
have prevented any prosecution. On December 17, 2003,
former Governor George Ryan was indicted on federal
charges of taking payoffs in return for government con-
tracts and leases. He was the 66th person indicted in the
investigation by the U.S. Attorney for the Northern District of Illinois. His defense attorney, Daniel Webb,
vowed there would be no plea bargaining. They intend
to fight the case on its merits and win approval of their
not-guilty plea. It's hard to believe that any novelist
would have asked readers to swallow such jaw-dropping
irony—that the man who traveled across Europe from

the British Parliament to the Reichstag, accepting the highest praise that they could bestow upon the most "courageous man in America," including a Nobel Peace Prize nomination, would face the prospect of going to jail.

In summary, like George Ryan, I have looked at the recent wave of death penalty exonerations and asked, How could this have happened? What I have concluded is that there are hundreds of tiny decisions made in the course of investigation and trial that can easily be as wrong as they are right. Observers outside the criminal justice system assume that those decisions are based on centuries of precedents, ensuring that the guilty are punished and that the innocent never will be. But what those many tiny decisions really show us is the fragility of the system. The administration of justice is complicated, too complicated to make death its product.

ACKNOWLEDGMENTS

The idea for this book arose during the production of *Death Penalty on Trial*, a special program produced by Kurtis Productions for the A&E Television Network Series *Investigative Reports*. Sharon Barrett was the producer, Ariadne Gallagher and Karen Cooper were the associate producers, and Jude Leak was the editor.

Ari and Karen and Aysha Akmal canvassed more than one hundred exoneration cases which were crucial to my look at the death penalty. My thanks to Washburn University School of Law Distinguished Professor James A. Ahrens. Washburn law student Brette Hart assisted in his review of the manuscript.

Editor Kate Darnton contributed a much appreciated guiding hand, and attorneys Chris Plourd and Thomas Leslie provided insight and transcripts for the cases included in this book.

I am also indebted to Donna LaPietra for her skilled editor's eye and long hours of understanding and invaluable support.

There are many reporters and lawyers who have toiled over the death penalty longer than I. They have produced the data that have led to reforms. This book is but one more voice in the growing chorus questioning capital punishment in America.

INDEX

PublicAffairs is a publishing house founded in 1997. It is a tribute to the standards, values, and flair of three persons who have served as mentors to countless reporters, writers, editors, and book people of all kinds, including me.

I. F. STONE, proprietor of I. F. Stone's Weekly, combined a commitment to the First Amendment with entrepreneurial zeal and reporting skill and became one of the great independent journalists in American history. At the age of eighty, Izzy published The Trial of Socrates, which was a national bestseller. He wrote the book after he taught himself ancient Greek.

BENJAMIN C. BRADLEE was for nearly thirty years the charismatic editorial leader of The Washington Post. It was Ben who gave the Post the range and courage to pursue such historic issues as Watergate. He supported his reporters with a tenacity that made them fearless and it is no accident that so many became authors of influential, best-selling books.

ROBERT L. BERNSTEIN, the chief executive of Random House for more than a quarter century, guided one of the nation's premier publishing houses. Bob was personally responsible for many books of political dissent and argument that challenged tyranny around the globe. He is also the founder and longtime chair of Human Rights Watch, one of the most respected human rights organizations in the world.

For fifty years, the banner of Public Affairs Press was carried by its owner Morris B. Schnapper, who published Gandhi, Nasser, Toynbee, Truman, and about 1,500 other authors. In 1983, Schnapper was described by The Washington Post as "a redoubtable gadfly." His legacy will endure in the books to come.

Peter Osnos, Publisher